REVIEWS

"...comprehensive and well written..."—University of Michigan's Consumer Web Site

"...provides invaluable ammunition for the shopper, whether you intend to lease or buy."—*Autoweek* (November 5, 1990)

"...one of the best books for the car buyer is one about leasing."—*Kiplinger's Personal Finance Magazine* (July 1995)

HOW TO SAVE
BIG
MONEY
WHEN YOU LEASE A CAR

Michael Flinn

A Perigee Book

A Perigee Book
Published by The Berkley Publishing Group
A member of Penguin Putnam Inc.
375 Hudson Street
New York, New York 10014

First edition: July 1990
Revised edition: April 1999

Published simultaneously in Canada.

The Penguin Putnam Inc. World Wide Web site address is
http://www.penguinputnam.com

Library of Congress Cataloging-in-Publication Data

Flinn, Michael, 1943–
    How to save big money when you lease a car / Michael Flinn. —
1st ed.
        p. cm.
    "A Perigee book."
    Includes index.
    ISBN 0-399-52483-5
    1. Automobile leasing and renting—United States—Popular works.
I. Title.
    HE5620.R45 F57 1999
    629.222'029'7—dc21   98-32329
                                                          CIP

Printed in the United States of America

10 9 8 7 6 5 4 3 2 1

*This book is dedicated to
the memory of my mother and father.*

CONTENTS

HOW TO SAVE
BIG
MONEY
WHEN YOU LEASE A CAR

INTRODUCTION

Leasing is a way to drive and enjoy a brand-new car and yet make a low, even amazingly low, monthly payment. It's also a way for the friendly folks at your local car store to take you for a long and mysterious ride—at the end of which you say good-bye to a whole lot of money. Many people who lease cars spend hundreds, even thousands of dollars more than necessary to drive the car they want.

The reason is simple: ignorance. Most people know less about leasing a car than about any other common, everyday consumer transaction. Unfortunately, in the car business, consumer ignorance generates money. When you are short on knowledge, you get taken for the long dollar.

Why don't people catch on? *Low payments*. Lease payments are normally so much lower than buy payments that they seduce customers into a state of bliss, blinding them to the ton of markup that can be hidden in that low payment.

My Credentials — and a Quote from the Boss

In addition to many months of research for this and earlier editions of the book, I sold and leased cars at a Ford dealer during the mid- to late-eighties. I played a small part in the creation of a gigantic consumer phenomenon, for at that time Ford was pioneering mass consumer auto leasing. The dealership I worked for, called herein the East Babbitt Ford Store, was located in the corner of a big Northeastern state. Within a fifteen minute drive of the place there were *eight* other Ford dealerships. The closest was only five minutes away. One of the others had been for years — and still is — the highest volume Ford dealer in that very large state. Competition was so intense that the area was a car shopper's paradise. In the face of that competition we were, month in and month out, either second or third in Ford sales in the region.

The things I'll be telling you about will be things I learned — and did — at a high-powered, high-volume dealership. And we loved leasing. Because, in the face of all that competition, it enabled us to make more money. As the general manager of the dealership put it (several times): "The great thing about leasing is, they (the customers) can never figure it out."

For the most part, he was right. And he was not talking about people who didn't know their ears from their elbows, as a couple of incidents may show.

True Stories

John

John was around thirty. Newly married, he was in the market for a station wagon. When he came into the store, I found him a Taurus wagon he liked and sold him on it. Then we sat down to negotiate the lease.

John worked as a manager for a copy machine store, and because copy machines are often leased, I figured I'd have a problem. I did.

The negotiation stretched over three days; John made three separate trips to the store. In the end, I leased him the wagon for $269 over dealer cost, giving up about $1,500 worth of profit, and about $300 worth of commission.

This deal was long and tough and I didn't make all that much money. But John knew what he was doing, so he didn't need to get defensive or hostile, and the deal was pleasant all the way through. We parted on friendly terms.

This can be important, and here's why: Later on, John had trouble with the wagon's front stereo speakers. When he came in to get them fixed, the service department gave him a runaround. He asked me to help. I listened to them, spoke to the service manager and solved the problem in ten minutes. And I was happy to do it. Without my intervention, it could have taken him two weeks, three visits, and a couple of arguments to get himself a new pair of speakers.

Paul

On the other hand, there was Paul, also a nice guy. Paul wanted a pickup truck. He was in his midtwenties, was ambitious, had a side business and not much money. Ooooh, I thought, Paul needs a super deal—he needs a lease.

We didn't have the truck he wanted, so he also needed to order it from the factory. I wrote up the order then explained leasing to him. I told him that, due to a special leasing program, I would discount the truck $2,000.

Whoa! He thought this was a super deal, and didn't even

question why I was giving him the truck below cost. He took the deal, and I did the paperwork, showing a $2,000 discount and a lease payment.

When the truck arrived, I called him and he came by to look at it before taking delivery. It was a gorgeous summer Saturday afternoon, around closing time. The only people left in the dealership were me and the owner's son-in-law, who also functioned as the F&I Guy.

Paul loved the truck, but Paul no longer loved the deal. While waiting for the truck, he had sensed that something was wrong. Now he was suspicious, challenging.

I took him up to the podium where the managers sat — a secret place. I introduced him to the owner's son-in-law. He was not appeased. So we began to show him the secrets of auto financing. We spent an hour with him. Almost the whole time he was suspicious and hostile. But we kept on, in a very friendly manner, showing him things. We showed him loan payment charts, we showed him factor charts with and without credit insurance, we showed him leasing charts, we showed him loan amortization charts, we showed him how to figure out the remaining balance on a loan.

When it was all over, he was no longer hostile. We had proved to his complete satisfaction that he had indeed gotten a $2,000 discount on the truck. He was convinced that he had wangled what was damn near the deal of the century. He went away happy and when he came in to take delivery he was still happy.

The actual price of the truck was $500 over sticker.

Paul was no dummy. In fact, his intelligence had given him an insight into something about which most customers remained clueless. "These numbers don't seem right," he thought. He simply lacked the knowledge to back up that insight.

The only difference between these customers was that John knew about leasing; Paul didn't. When you lease a car, knowledge is truly power.

THE PURPOSE OF THIS BOOK

The purpose of this book, then, is simple: to provide you with the knowledge that will help you save money if you lease a car. The book will help you understand what you are doing — and what is being done to you — and how to handle whatever is being done to you. The book will also:

- · Define leasing's important terms
- · Answer the most commonly asked questions about leasing
- · Acquaint you with the numbers and formulae used in lease deals; tell you where to find them, how to use them, and how to figure some of them out from scratch
- · Show you how to decide what to do, and not just tell you what to do
- · Provide guidelines to help you determine the value of your trade-in, and of used cars in general
- · Show you how to negotiate a good deal
- · Describe in detail some of the tricks and scams salespeople will try to play on you, and teach you how to turn them to your advantage

When you lease a car, as when you buy a car, almost everything is negotiable. Therefore, anything you do not ask for or negotiate for will not be offered to you. With this book, you will know what to ask for and how to get it. Your savings could be from $100 to $2,000 or even more.

I have also tried to provide sufficient detail so that if

something goes wrong, you'll be able to figure out what went wrong and how to fix it. Read carefully, and you should have a pretty good idea what's going on, and what to do if something goes wrong, throughout the entire process of leasing.

A Word on the Examples

Some of the examples of lease deals and lease payments I use are not necessarily the best deals available. I don't want to sell you on the idea of leasing; I want to sell you on the idea that a little work and a little learning will do you a whole lot of good if and when you do lease.

Nor am I recommending the cars in the examples, as the best cars available or the best cars to lease. In general economic terms, the best cars to lease are the same as the best cars to buy: those whose reputations for quality, reliability, and durability give them high residual values, which, in turn, makes the monthly lease payment low in relation to the price. But you're going to be driving a car, not a residual value or a monthly payment. So the car for you is the car that turns you on, or the car that suits your needs.

The principles of leasing do not change from car to car. They are the same for a Kia or a Hyundai, a Honda or a Ford Explorer, a Cadillac or a Mercedes. However, some of the things you need to know will be specific to your time and place, like the value of your old car and the dealer cost of the new car. Although I can't tell you such things in advance, I will tell you how to discover them for yourself. And do take the trouble to discover them. To make your best deal, you have to do your homework.

ONE

WHAT'S LEASING ALL ABOUT?

Let's begin with a bird's-eye view of the whole process and some useful definitions. In some ways, leasing and buying are quite similar. You make a deal; that is, you agree on an amount of money to be paid for a car and sign a contract. A lender, usually a bank, a savings and loan, or an auto manufacturer's credit company, advances that money and you drive away in the car. You pay back that sum of money — plus interest — in regular monthly payments. The main differences are:

- The number of legal controls government has placed on the transaction. Leasing has fewer.
- The time it takes for you to pay back the amount you owe. With leasing, you pay back much more slowly.
- The degree of risk taken by the lender. Leasing is considered riskier. First, there can be more money at stake, for leasing can generate higher profits than installment

loans. Also, whatever the profit, the lender waits longer to recover both the profit and the original amount invested in the loan.

When you mix these differences and shake gently, the result is leasing's major drawback in comparison to buying.

If you pay off a buy loan early, most installment purchase contracts require you to pay only the remaining principal: what's left of the original amount lent to you. The uncollected interest is foregone.

But if you end a lease before the term is up, many lessors will apply charges over and above the amount they originally spent, which usually equals the purchase price of the car. In cases of early termination, lease contracts often specify that you pay some or all of the remaining interest charges, plus a penalty, plus some or all of the car's future estimated value. Later, we'll discuss excessive charges for early termination in more detail and talk about how to minimize them.

Despite the differences between leasing and buying, a leased car is a sold car. The dealer submits the lease contract to the lessor and is paid cash. The dealer pays off whoever financed the car, whether it be the manufacturer or a bank, and has the rest for profit. Or, if you trade a car in, he has your trade to sell for profit. The leased car is gone; the dealer is rid of all responsibility for it.

Except, that is, in some cases when the dealer, acting as an agent of the lessor, receives the car when you turn it in. Then he fills out a report describing the car's condition and collects any money you owe the lessor for damage or for mileage that exceeds the agreement.

In return for acting as the lessor's agent, the dealer gains the opportunity to sell the car, to you or to someone else, as a used car, for as much profit as he can get. However, the dealer is not required to sell the car, or to repair the car, or to wash and wax the car, or anything else.

When the lease expires, the lessor (almost always the financing agency involved) owns the car. If the dealer cannot or will not sell it, the financing agency must take the responsibility and risk of realizing the money represented by the car's residual value. Residual value simply means the estimated dollar value of the car when the lease expires; an estimate made at the beginning of the lease.

From your point of view as a customer, when you lease a car, you buy the use of it for a certain amount of time. That time equals a certain percentage of the car's "life expectancy." And that time is convertible to a certain percentage of the car's monetary value, or retail price. You pay x dollars to buy a certain percentage of the car's life. To this, interest and taxes are added, but basically this all adds up to lower payments. You pay for only that portion of the car's life which you use. Since this is considerably less than the full value of the car, in most states you also pay less in sales tax.

STATE SALES TAX "BREAKS"

Some states tax leases the way they should be taxed, at least in part. In those states, you pay sales, or "use," tax on the amount of your payment. The tax is due each month. You pay the lessor and the lessor passes it along to the state or county. This provides you with two benefits.

One is that, even though you're paying taxes on finance charges, which should be illegal, the tax on payments normally amounts to a lot less money than you'd pay on a buy.

The other is that, because it's collected month by month rather than all at once, this tax does not have to be taken from your bank account, which would leave you with less money and lower your interest income. Nor does the tax have to be financed, which would, of course, add to the interest you must pay.

But since politicians eternally seek more money, some states have moved to eliminate the advantage of paying the sales tax month by month, an advantage that leasing should provide. New York, for example, has decided that the total tax on the sum of the payments is due when you make the deal. So, you either pay the tax up front—which takes more money out of your pocket (or your interest-bearing account)—or you finance the amount of the tax—which adds an interest charge that previously did not apply.

Pennsylvania, on the other hand, came up with a different strategy. Sales taxes are still due with the monthly payment. But the law was changed so that individual counties may add lease surcharges. As a result, although the state sales tax is 6 percent, if you lease a car in, say, Montgomery County, you pay 9 percent. In Philadelphia County, you pay 10 percent.

I don't have enough space to consider tax practices state by state or county by county. Check to determine the lease tax laws in your own area.

Federal Tax Laws

As you know, federal income tax is an underworld of confusion, about which unlicensed citizens are forbidden to speak. So let me say only this: many people seem to think that leasing a car offers you a super-write-off on your income tax. As far as I can tell, however, from the IRS's badly written rules, the advantage is slim to none.

Proportionally, your write-offs for business use of your car seem to be similar whether you lease or buy. For example, if you write off a large percentage of your lease payment for business use of your car, you may have to add an "inclusion amount" to your gross income. The IRS flatly states that the purpose of the inclusion amount is to prevent your deduction for lease payments from exceeding the deduction for depreciation you could take if you were buying the car. So before jumping to any conclusions about the tax advantage of leasing, check with a professional tax advisor.

One federal tax wrinkle that favored ordinary, nonbusiness buyers, however, no longer exists. You can no longer write off interest paid on consumer purchase loans, so that particular tax advantage to buying a car is gone.

And now let's take a quick peek at the strange world of financial law. To paraphrase a famous injunction: Ask not what the law will do for you; ask instead what you must do to benefit from the law.

FREQUENTLY ASKED QUESTIONS ABOUT LEASING

WHO LEASES?

Anybody who wants or needs to. Once upon a time, leasing was considered the thing to do mainly for doctors, lawyers, business owners, and corporations. But now leasing is simply another method of mass consumer auto financing. Anybody and everybody does it. From my friend the mortgage processor, a guy in his midtwenties . . .

. . . to a middle-aged parochial school teacher who had never had a new car in her life and who was ready to wipe

out her savings account so she could afford buy payments . . .

   . . . to a young woman in the computer business who
made good money but wanted to put out as little of it as
possible and still have a super-fancy compact sport truck . . .

   . . . to a successful pig farmer who wanted to cruise the
countryside in a full-sized, four-wheel-drive pickup truck
that was loaded to the max.

   Current estimates indicate that over four million people
a year lease cars. The numbers are difficult to pinpoint because auto manufacturers record leases as retail sales.

WHY LEASE?

To get lower monthly payments. Or to get a larger or fancier
car for the same payment. Or to speed the trade cycle, that
is, to get a new car more frequently, while keeping payments
lower than they would be if you purchased a new car every
two or three years. Car companies, most notably Ford, began to promote mass consumer leasing in the mid eighties,
when rising prices and high interest rates were putting new
car payments beyond the reach of many people. With leasing, you pay less because you pay only for that part of the
life value of the car that you use up.

   Thus a new car becomes affordable. And, in some states,
where the payment for a leased car does not show up as a
debt on credit reports, you can get a new car and still have
those thousands of dollars of credit available. These are real
and substantial benefits.

   And if you know how to negotiate a good deal on a lease,
you will get these benefits for less than they are worth, even
if leasing costs you a few hundred more than the best case
scenario on a buy.

Let me emphasize this, because it's often overlooked in newspaper and magazine articles.

1. There is no predeterminable total cost to lease or buy a car. Too many variables come into play—not the least of which is you and your habits. So when you see one of those sidebar charts purporting to show the overall costs of leasing versus buying, take it with a grain of salt. However, after working through the examples in the following chapters, you'll learn how to make an educated guesstimate—in terms of your own circumstances.

2. When you put out less money than it usually costs to do something (like leasing a car, or buying a house with a no-point mortgage or a low down payment) so that you can free up money to do another thing, you can end up paying more in the long run.

However, this is simply irrelevant if you must do both things, or if doing both things will enable your money to earn you a greater return.

And that's how you should think about it. Not: Will it cost me $587 more if I start out by leasing then decide to buy the car in the end? But: What will I get in return if it does cost me more? Suppose the monthly saving allows you to furnish your living room two years sooner than you would otherwise be able to? Suppose it allows you to invest $100 a month in a penny stock you are convinced is going to skyrocket?

Let me also say, however, that—as with all credit decisions—you should carefully consider your present and future ability to pay.

Is Leasing Good for Me if My Credit Is Bad?

No. In general, you need better credit to lease than you do to buy on time. Why? Because not only is the lender trusting you to repay the money, they are also trusting you to return the car in reasonably good shape. Since they're trusting you more, it takes less to scare them away.

However, many lenders will permit cosigners on a lease and your income does not have to be as high as you may have heard. Some lenders stipulate a minimum income of $25,000 a year. Others, however, will be satisfied if you earn $16,000, and sometimes the manufacturer's credit companies will be satisfied with even less, if there is a creditworthy cosigner.

Who Pays for Insurance and Nonwarranty Repairs?

You do. Most leases make you responsible for insuring and repairing the car.

Does the Manufacturer's Warranty Cover a Leased Car?

Yes. You receive all the protection the warranty affords. This is also true with any extended warranties you may purchase. Drivers who will put on less than sixty thousand miles during the lease term probably don't need an extended warranty. Drivers who will drive more than sixty thousand during the lease may save money with an extended warranty.

A tip: if your car is loaded with motor-driven options, see if the manufacturer's warranty will cover them for the term of your lease. If it doesn't, try to find out how often they break on that model. If many of these options have a reputation for breaking often and early, check the price of an extended warranty that covers them. You will have some time to do this; most extended warranty plans can be purchased up to twelve months after you take the car.

DOES LEASING REQUIRE ME TO CARRY MORE INSURANCE?

Generally speaking, no. . . . But: most leases have an insurance requirement of $50,000 property damage and $100/300,000 bodily injury liability insurance, and comprehensive and collision insurance with a maximum deductible of $500.

In areas of the country where auto insurance is not tremendously expensive, this is pretty much a standard policy, the policy that most people have.

In areas like Philadelphia, however, where auto insurance is tremendously expensive, buying on an installment loan may enable you to save money on insurance. Installment purchase contracts require you to carry insurance; in fact, most require the same coverage as a lease. But some purchase contracts do not specify the amounts of required coverage. And many lenders do not check to see if you have any at all. On a buy, you may be able to get away with reducing your coverage and save a significant amount of money. Unless, of course, you have a serious accident.

Check insurance costs in your area for different amounts of coverage. Check with local lenders to find out how much coverage is required on their installment purchase contracts. Then check with the department of motor vehicles to see what your state requires. The state may have a requirement that overrides any differences between lease and purchase contracts.

Do Low Factory Finance Rates and Cash Rebates Always Apply When You Lease?

Interest rate buydowns (below-market financing) sometimes apply only to purchase loans. But as car prices continue to rise dramatically, manufacturers' credit companies are subsidizing leases more often. Ask about factory lease programs at the dealership. For if the factory is not running (i.e., paying for) an advertising program, some dealers may not tell you about the subsidy. Dealers prefer the lender who pays them the most, whether or not it costs you more.

Cash rebates, on the other hand, usually come with the car, not the method of financing. Lease or buy, you get the rebate. And since the cash comes from the manufacturer, the rebate applies whether you lease from a dealership or a lease store.

Factory cash is your money; the factory pays it to you. This means that you decide how to use it. You can sign the check over to the dealer and use it as cash down to lower your lease payment. Or you can walk out of the store with the check in your pocket. You can even use it to lower the lease buyout, if you know that you'll be buying the car later—although in most cases this would be a bad idea. Money now is worth more than money later.

If you can handle the payment without putting money down, think of the rebate as money in the bank, able to earn interest for you. Compare what you will earn with what you'll save if you put it down on the car (see chapter 4).

But Won't I Be Better Off Owning the Car?

It depends on the meaning of "own" and of "better off."

This question is usually voiced as an objection or a complaint. The complaint has two parts. First, the person feels that he or she will be deprived of the pride of ownership. But neither he nor she nor you will own the car anyway. The feeling of ownership is basically science fiction: a form of time travel. One projects oneself into a happy future when all the payments have been made.

If you are buying on time, you must pay off the loan and obtain a lien release before you own the car. As long as your car is under lien, the lienholder owns it.

And not only does the lienholder have the right to take the car away from you if you fail to make your payments, they can also tell you what to do with the car while you're making them.

Here are a few examples, taken from the back side of a typical bank installment purchase contract:

- You must keep the car insured, policies payable to the bank.
- You may not transfer, abandon, or substantially modify the car without written consent from the bank.
- You may not remove the car from the state for more than one month without written consent from the bank.
- You may not move to another state without written consent from the bank.

Think that one over, folks.

"Own" the car? When you sign up to "buy" the car on time, you lose ownership of yourself. You lose some of your rights as an American citizen. Of course, this is unconstitutional. But how much would it cost to prove it?

The Idea of Ownership, Part Two: Equity

For all practical purposes, equity is simply the amount of money you can get for something over and above what you owe on it and what it costs you to sell it. What you get minus what you pay for debt and selling costs equals your equity—whether the object be a house, a car, or a pair of underpants.

The second part of the idea of ownership is that when you buy on time you can recover some of your money by cashing in the equity your payments have built up in the vehicle.

But the value of most cars declines rapidly. The equity built up through monthly buy payments may be less than you expect and must be compared to the "equity in cash" achieved by the monthly savings of a lease.

CAN YOU HAVE EQUITY IN A LEASED VEHICLE?

Yes. And if you have it, you can cash it in—as long as the lease has a purchase option. If, however, the lease purchase price, or buyout, is high, you may have little hope of realizing any profit. If you have to pay the lessor a high price for the car, you'll have to sell it for a very high price in order to make any money.

Selling a leased car is the same as selling any car that is under lien. A month or two before the lease is up, find out the amount of the lease payoff and compare it to the amount you can get for the car. If you can get more than you have to pay (assuming you have a closed-end lease with an option to buy) you sell the car, pay off the lease, and pocket the profit.

If you can't, you turn the car in.

THE SECURITY DEPOSIT—HOW MUCH? IS IT NEGOTIABLE?

The refundable security deposit secures the lessor against damage or excessive wear and tear to the car. On Ford, GMAC, Nissan Credit, and Toyota Credit leases, the amount deposited has traditionally been the amount of the payment rounded upward to the nearest multiple of twenty-five. With a lease payment of $174.00 your security deposit would be $175. Some lessors ask for more: payment plus $100, payment plus $200, or a flat $400 to $500. The deposit is refundable, but the more cash you spend up front, the more you cut into the advantage you seek from leasing in the first place. The function of leasing is to keep more cash at your disposal. The security deposit may be negotiable and it's worth a try, but don't count on it. Instead, go after a lower payment.

Suppose you've made a deal for price and payment, then find out the lender wants a big security deposit. Tell the salesperson that GM and Ford require deposits of payment rounded to the next highest multiple of twenty-five. So if you have to put out a higher security deposit, you want a lower payment.

Suppose the amount is $100 more than GMAC requires. Over three years, you could lose about $25 to $30 in interest. So, on a 36-month lease, the payment should drop $1.00 a month. Right? By the way, if you prefer not to put out cash, the dealer should be able to get the security deposit financed. If the lease rate is low, it may be worth doing. The lower the lease rate, the more worth doing it is.

Here's how to decide:

Find out how much higher your lease payment will be if you finance the security deposit. Multiply the overage by the number of payments in the lease. Take the resulting total and subtract the amount of the security deposit. The remainder will be what you would pay in finance charges.

Now compare the finance charges with what the money would earn in interest over the term of the lease.

A *Financing Wrinkle to Check For*

Security deposits and other extra costs can be financed two different ways.

(a) They can be rolled into the capitalized cost of the car and subjected to the interest rate that applies to the lease. Or

(b) they can be calculated with a separate—and higher—interest rate and then added to the payment. (a) is preferable if the interest rate is lower, and it often is.

CAN YOU TRADE IN YOUR OLD CAR WHEN YOU LEASE A NEW ONE?

As salespeople like to say, Nooooo problem.

Whatever your car is worth beyond what you owe on it (your equity) will be deducted from the acquisition cost or capitalized cost of the leased car.

To put it another way, the trade equity will be deducted from the amount you finance on the lease. If you trade in a car worth $2,000 that you owned free and clear on a new car that you are leasing for say, four years, your payment would drop $40 to $50 a month. Plus the tax on that $40 to $50.

Can You Trade In a Leased Car?

Nooooo problem. Just like a buy. If the car is worth more than the payoff on the lease, that's your equity. It's credited against the new lease just like a cash down payment.

Can You Take Your Equity in Cash?

In all probability, yes. If your credit is good and you want your trade equity in cash, most dealers will hand you a check. But should you? There are two views to consider:

1. If lease rates are low and you can afford the higher payment, it may be worthwhile to take the cash. Consider it in the light of our discussion of cash down payments (chapter 4).

2. However, paying you cash for your equity can be used as a pressure tactic, a way to push you into dealing fast, dealing now, with no further negotiation. For instance: "I can put you in the Glitzmobile for two-ninety a month, right now, today, and cut you a check for nine hundred seventy-nine dollars. You can drive out of here in a brand new car, with a thousand dollars in your pocket."

If you hear something like this before you have agreed on the deal you want, do yourself a favor. Ignore the vision of dollars dancing in your head.

Can You Trade In a (Leased or Other) Car with Negative Equity?

You sure can. Your negative equity (the amount you owe beyond what your car is worth) is simply added to the price of the new car and you pay it off with your monthly payments. You can do this on a lease or a buy.

Many banks, however, will not want your paper if you do. But the factory credit companies are another story. They won't mind—as long as your credit is good and the amount of your negative equity does not push the balance on the new car too, too far beyond its value.

This is an important point to remember. In many situations, the manufacturer's credit arm will put a higher priority on selling the manufacturer's car than on making a perfectly sensible loan, the way a bank would. This can help you escape from an unreliable used car for which you owe more than you can get. But it can also help you bury yourself forever in the new car.

CAN YOU HAVE NEGATIVE EQUITY AFTER YOU'VE MADE THE LEASE PAYMENTS FOR THE FULL TERM?

No, you cannot. With two exceptions.

1. You bring the car back damaged. As noted earlier, it's your responsibility to pay for repairs. If somebody hits your car with a hammer, spend the insurance check to fix it.

2. You made the mistake of signing an open-end lease. Some of these can sound good. "Look at this," the salesperson tells you. "You can collect the profit when the lease expires. If it's worth more than we thought it would be, we'll pay you the difference. You could really make out."

Sure you could. This is a lousy gamble. There's only a slight chance that the car will be worth more than the original estimate when you turn it in. And there's a very good chance that it will be worth less than the original estimate. If less, you pay the difference.

I Want to Own My Car and Keep It Forever. Can Leasing Help Me in Any Way?

Yes, because leasing will put you into more car for a lower payment. You could then treat the lease as a buy with an extended term. When the lease expired, you could finance the buyout for two or three more years.

Obviously, this means a longer loan, more interest paid, and more money out of pocket in the long run. Is this bad? Not necessarily. The lower payment might make it possible for you to have the car that suits your needs rather than the car that you can afford.

Should I Lease a Used Car?

Used car leases have become much more common in the last few years, particularly on luxury cars like Mercedes and Lexus. Is it worth it?

If the residual value used to calculate the payment on the used car is high enough, and the lease (interest) rate is low enough, yes. For the residual value to be high, the car will have to have a reputation for quality, reliability, and durability.

Some cars do. But watch out. An intelligent but inexperienced customer I know leased a one-year-old, very fancy Mercury Cougar based on a price that was about $1,200 less than the price of the car brand new. The car was actually worth $4,000 less than the brand new car. So while payment seemed low, it was, in fact, very high.

Chapter 5 shows how to calculate lease payments; from this you will be able to determine whether or not a leased used car is any kind of bargain. Chapter 10 has an example that illustrates the differences between computing payments on new and used cars.

Do I Need a Computer and a Software Package to Calculate Lease Payments?

No. The ones I've seen range in price from $30 to $269. You need them only if you cannot add, subtract, multiply, and divide—with a five-dollar calculator. In the auto business, the computers are there to confuse you. But you can't fight their computers with your computer. Their computer costs more; their software is better.

What you can fight their computer with is a piece of paper, a pencil, and simple arithmetic. The fact is, once you understand them, lease payments are not all that hard to figure out. But you do need to understand them. The new consumer leasing law offers help, but it won't rescue the ignorant. The law helps those who help themselves.

What Do You Do When the Lease Is Up?

You bring the car back to the dealer or lease store you got it from, then either buy it or give it back. If you give it back, the store then either sells it or arranges to return it to the lender/lessor. The car you bring back is supposed to be in "average" condition for its age. If not, you forfeit whatever part of your security deposit is needed to bring it into average condition. And more, if it takes more.

At the place I worked, and, I believe, at most car stores, average means average. Normally, a dealer will not be as harsh a judge of the condition of your car as would, say, a bank: the dealer wants to lease you another car, not have you stomp off the lot swearing at him over a couple hundred dollars.

Among other things, "average" means:

· The car should have tires that will pass inspection. (Sometimes expressed as tread one-eighth inch deep.)
· The light bulbs should all be there and working, as should the radio that came with the car, and everything else that came with the car. You are not supposed to take the jack and the spare tire as going-away presents to yourself.
· The sheet metal is not supposed to be bent, folded, or mutilated. Nicks and dings are generally O.K. But if you smack the car, you are supposed to spend your insurance check to get it fixed, not to finance a trip to Aruba.
· The exhaust system is supposed to be on the car, not completely rotted out.
· The window glass is not supposed to be cracked or smashed.

"Average condition" is pretty much a matter of common sense. It's not perfect. Neither is it smashed up or with parts missing. But read your lease contract carefully before signing it. Make sure it contains no zingers about the condition of the car.

Zingers: Who Pays?

You pay. Here are some zingers that could cost you hundreds of dollars:

· New or "good" tires as opposed to inspectable tires.
· "Good retail condition" instead of average condition.

(There is no such thing as "good retail condition" or "decent retail condition." There is extra clean, clean, average, and rough (with mileage and options adjustments). Yet I have seen the aforementioned "good retail" and "decent retail" condition in lease contracts. These phrases could be interpreted as clean, and the difference between average and clean starts at about $500 and rises to $5,000 or even more.)

· No body rust permitted in an area of the country where rust is common, if not inevitable.

· A requirement that you pay to repair faulty power window mechanisms and other electronic malfunctions. Watch out for this. It suggests that the lessor expects the power doodads to break shortly after the warranty expires. Power doodads are very expensive to repair.

There may be others. Check carefully.

IN WHAT WAY IS LEASING LIKE BUYING A CAR?

In both, almost everything is negotiable. It's important to realize that, therefore, anything you do not ask for or negotiate for will not be offered to you.

HOW WELL DOES THE LAW PROTECT YOU?

Two laws are in place that can help protect you when it comes to leasing. The first is the Consumer Credit Act of 1976. This was the landmark legislation that required lenders to disclose points and other fees on loans, along with the true annualized interest rate, or APR. The second law is the Consumer Leasing Act of 1996. Regulation M, the section specifying the rules and regulations, went into effect in January 1998. Regulation M adds some badly needed, but not quite sufficient, consumer protection.

The original, the Consumer Credit Act of 1976, grants lessees some protection, but not enough. The act unreasonably differentiates between installment purchases and leases. (And so does Regulation M.) Why? Either the writers of the legislation did not fully understand time as a commodity or suave lobbyists whispered honeyed words. You see, for a lease to be considered a "credit sale" and thus for the lessee to receive the full protection of the law, the lessee must pay a sum at least as great as the value of the property.

Now, it is indeed possible to pay that much. The point, however, is not to pay that much. The point is to have and use the car during its best years, while paying a sum less than its full value. So leasing can never be considered a credit sale as long as there's a good reason to do it.

In the practical world, however, auto leasing is nothing but a credit sale: another way to finance a car. The only close analogy to "renting" that I can think of is a real estate lease/purchase deal. And even that analogy is faulty.

Leasing a car is not like renting real estate. A building will go on existing into the indefinite future. But a car has a very limited and predictable life span. You are buying a fraction of that life and a fairly accurate numerical value can be put on that fraction. And you are, at least potentially, building equity, which can be cashed in.

In the legal world, however, the lessor is renting you property rather than selling you time or a known fraction of the life of a commodity. From the lessor's point of view, this is a good thing. The lessor receives additional tax breaks. And, at the same time, its responsibility to you decreases. For renters tend to have reduced status in the eyes of the law.

Under the Consumer Credit Act, when you leased a car:

- · The lessor did not have to disclose the actual interest rate you were being charged.
- · The lessor did not have to divulge its true estimate of what the vehicle's future value would be when the lease expired.

· The lessor did not have to tell you the actual balance owed when the lease expires.

Since essential information could be withheld, you could be easily conned. Think about that last little fact above. Suppose that, after paying your mortgage for five years, the bank would not tell you what you still owed on your house. Instead, you had to ask the person who sold it to you. Then you paid whatever that person said, and they paid off the bank. Would that person add a few buckaroos for herself? It's conceivable, isn't it. Now, what if that person were a car dealer?

The original act did give you some protection. The lessor was (and still is, under the new law—the Consumer Leasing Act) legally required to state:

· That the lease is a lease (i.e., that you must return the car).
· How much cash, if any, must be paid up front.
· The number of payments and the total amount of those payments.
· Your liability, if any, for the difference between estimated and actual market value of the vehicle at the end of the lease.
· If you do have such liability, how the amount will be determined.
· Whether or not you have an option to purchase; and, if so, at what time and at what price.

REGULATION M

Regulation M reprises the previous law's requirements and adds some of its own. It also demands greater specificity from the lessor when listing charges you are obligated to pay and greater clarity in the language of lease contracts.

Surprisingly, it also exhibits a bit of common sense and puts it into action. Regulation M stipulates that when it provides greater consumer protection than state law, it overrides state law; but when state law provides greater consumer protection, the state law prevails.

Here's a summary of the new legislation. Parenthetical remarks indicate what I sense will be shortcomings. The seller or lessor must disclose to you:

- A description of the property.
- The amount due at lease signing, with each separate component itemized.
- The payment, the number of payments, and the sum total of all the payments.
- Any other charges, in itemized form.
- The payment calculation, in detailed, itemized form, expressed in such a way that shows you how the payment was calculated. (If you ask for it to be itemized.)
- An Early Termination Statement, explaining the conditions under which you or the lessor may terminate the lease early, and a description of how the early termination charges will be calculated.
- An Early Termination Warning, stating that you may have to pay large amounts if you terminate early, including this warning: "The charge may be up to several thousand dollars."
- A statement of responsibility for maintenance and repair.
- A statement of wear and use standards, "which must be

reasonable." (This is too vague. What is the difference in your mind between "average condition" and "decent retail condition"? Most people probably wouldn't see much difference, but in fact it could be thousands of dollars.)

· A notice of the charge for excess mileage. (Usually included with reasonable amount of prominence.)

· Notice of purchase option with purchase price. (In the previous law.)

· A notice of any purchase option during the lease term — and the price or method of determining the price.

· A clear statement of your liability, if any, for the difference between the vehicle's estimated residual value and its realized value, which means, simply, the amount the lessor actually sells it for. (In the previous law.)

SHORTCOMINGS AND BENEFITS OF THE NEW LAW

Shortcomings

Although a step in the right direction, the new law still has several shortcomings that you need to be aware of. They are:

Redundancy— Many of the provisions of Regulation M were already included in the Consumer Credit Act of 1976.

Interest Rate Disclosure— The new law does not compel disclosure of the true interest rate in terms of APR or anything like APR. Leasing lobbyists argued against that disclosure, claiming that it could be used, in conjunction with manipulated residual values, to confuse consumers. They won the point with that argument. What the government did instead of compelling interest rate disclosure was to compel a warning: If an interest rate is advertised, there must be a disclaimer stating that the advertised rate may not reflect the true cost of the financing. You can calculate the interest rate on a lease and you can convert it into an APR. Or if you want to be a stickler for leasing lingo, you can convert it into a lease APR. But since nobody has to, nobody will.

Balance Owed Disclosure— As far as I can tell, Regulation M does not require the lessor to tell you the actual balance owed on the lease. What is the actual balance owed on a lease? It is the amount the dealer or lease store must pay the lessor if it wants to sell your leased car to you, or to anyone else, at the end of the lease. In many cases, you will never know what it is.

Disclosure Timing— The timing of the disclosure during the deal. Regulation M states: "A lessor shall provide the disclosures prior to the consummation of a consumer lease." That could mean two minutes before you sign the contract and drive off in the new car. By then, however, the salesperson could have you believing the moon is blue and that "gross capitalized cost" means something other than what the government's lawyers intended it to mean.

And that is precisely the scenario lessors are writing up. The Disclosure Form mandated by Regulation M has simply been incorporated into lease contracts. If you do not ask for it sooner, you won't see it until you come in to sign for and drive off in the car. At that moment, however, few people, including me, your friendly leasing expert, are capable of thinking very clearly.

For Regulation M to be as effective as possible, all disclosures should be made before or during negotiation. The actual Disclosure Form should have been required to be part of the purchase order form, or work sheet, the salesperson uses, with you, to work out the price and place the order for the car.

Confusing Jargon— Clumsy wording rears its confusing head. "Gross capitalized cost," "capitalized cost reduction," and "adjusted capitalized cost" are unnecessary and annoying accountant/lawyer versions of simple, one-syllable words.

Gross capitalized cost is nothing but the total price: the price of the car and the prices of anything else you buy with the car. *Capitalized cost reduction* is the phrase dealers and lessors use in ads in order to avoid the words "cash down" or "down payment." And the *adjusted capitalized cost* is simply the capitalized cost of the lease. That is, the money the lessor considers itself to have paid for the car—and usually has.

Restricted Application— The very peculiar restriction of the law's applicability to deals with a "contractual value" of $25,000 or less. This should be easy to change and, therefore, should be changed immediately.

Benefits

Now, on the plus side, Regulation M does have some valuable benefits. A very definite step in the right direction is that, even though some terms are vague enough to provide sales aids, the new law requires the lessor to reveal more of its methods, in more detail, than ever before. Particularly important (visible in the form below) are:

Federal Consumer Leasing Act Disclosure

Date _____

Lessor(s) _____   Lessee(s) _____

Amount Due at Lease Signing (Itemized below)*	Monthly Payments	Other Charges (not part of your monthly payment)	Total of Payments (The amount you will have paid by the end of the lease)
$ _____	Your first monthly payment of $ _____ is due on _____, followed by _____ payments of $ _____ due on the _____ of each month. The total of your monthly payments is $ _____.	Disposition fee (if you do not purchase the vehicle) $_____ [Annual tax] _____ Total $_____	$ _____

* Itemization of Amount Due at Lease Signing

Amount Due At Lease Signing:

		How the Amount Due at Lease Signing will be paid:	
Capitalized cost reduction	$ _____	Net trade-in allowance	$ _____
First monthly payment	_____	Rebates and noncash credits	_____
Refundable security deposit	_____	Amount to be paid in cash	_____
Title fees	_____		
Registration fees	_____		
_____ Total	$ _____	Total	$ _____

Your monthly payment is determined as shown below:

Gross capitalized cost. The agreed upon value of the vehicle ($ _____) and any items you pay over the lease term (such as service contracts, insurance, and any outstanding prior loan or lease balance) .... $ _____

If you want an itemization of this amount, please check this box. ☐

Capitalized cost reduction. The amount of any net trade-in allowance, rebate, noncash credit, or cash you pay that reduces the gross capitalized cost .... − _____

Adjusted capitalized cost. The amount used in calculating your base monthly payment .... = _____

Residual value. The value of the vehicle at the end of the lease used in calculating your base monthly payment .... − _____

Depreciation and any amortized amounts. The amount charged for the vehicle's decline in value through normal use and for other items paid over the lease term .... = _____

Rent charge. The amount charged in addition to the depreciation and any amortized amounts .... + _____

Total of base monthly payments. The depreciation and any amortized amounts plus the rent charge .... = _____

Lease term. The number of months in your lease .... ÷ _____

Base monthly payment .... = _____

Monthly sales/use tax .... + _____

_____ .... =$ _____

Total monthly payment ....

Early Termination. You may have to pay a substantial charge if you end this lease early. The charge may be up to several thousand dollars. The actual charge will depend on when the lease is terminated. The earlier you end the lease, the greater this charge is likely to be.

Excessive Wear and Use. You may be charged for excessive wear based on our standards for normal use [and for mileage in excess of _____ miles per year at the rate of _____ per mile].

Purchase Option at End of Lease Term. [You have an option to purchase the vehicle at the end of the lease term for $ _____ [and a purchase option fee of $ _____].] [You do not have an option to purchase the vehicle at the end of the lease term.]

Other Important Terms. See your lease documents for additional information on early termination, purchase options and maintenance responsibilities, warranties, late and default charges, insurance, and any security interest, if applicable.

a. The partial itemization of the payment calculation.
b. The requirement to stipulate the "types and amounts of insurance" acquired along with the lease.
c. The requirement to spell out the conditions under which you may terminate the lease before the term is over.

However, it behooves you to know what all these terms mean and how to figure them out for yourself. Here is the Disclosure Form that must be given to you before you complete the deal.

Description of Leased Property				
Year	Make	Model	Body Style	Vehicle I.D. #

[The following provisions are the nonsegregated disclosures required under Regulation M.]   Page 2 of 2

Official Fees and Taxes. The total amount you will pay for official and license fees, registration, title, and taxes over the term of your lease, whether included with your monthly payments or assessed otherwise: $ _____ .

Insurance. The following types and amounts of insurance will be acquired in connection with this lease:

_____ .

_____ We (lessor) will provide the insurance coverage quoted above for a total premium cost of $ _____ .

_____ You (lessee) agree to provide insurance coverage in the amount and types indicated above.

Standards for Wear and Use. The following standards are applicable for determining unreasonable or excess wear and use of the leased vehicle:

_____ .

Maintenance.
You are responsible for the following maintenance and servicing of the leased vehicle:

_____].

We are responsible for the following maintenance and servicing of the leased vehicle:

_____].

Warranties. The leased vehicle is subject to the following express warranties:

_____ .

Early Termination and Default. (a) You may terminate this lease before the end of the lease term under the following conditions:

_____ .

The charge for such early termination is:

_____ .

(b) We may terminate this lease before the end of the lease term under the following conditions:

_____ .

Upon such termination we shall be entitled to the following charge(s) for:

_____ .

(c) To the extent these charges take into account the value of the vehicle at termination, if you disagree with the value we assign to the vehicle, you may obtain, at your own expense, from an independent third party agreeable to both of us, a professional appraisal of the   value of the leased vehicle which could be realized at sale. The appraised value shall then be used as the actual value.

Security Interest. We reserve a security interest of the following type in the property listed below to secure performance of your obligations under this lease:

_____ .

Late Payments. The charge for late payments is: _____ .

Option to Purchase Leased Property Prior to the End of the Lease.   You have an option to purchase the leased vehicle prior to the end of the term. The price will be $ _____ / the method of determining the price. [You do not have an option to purchase the leased vehicle.]

Previously, the Consumer Credit Act protected you from the consumer equivalent of armed robbery. Now, the protection extends further. But my feeling is that, without requirements to disclose APR (true annualized interest rate), actual estimated lease-end value, and exact balance owed, Regulation M still allows you to be fast-talked, flim-flammed, and jived around, to the detriment of your bank account.

For example, take the last clause in the form above, regarding the option to purchase during the term. Suppose the salesperson writes in not the price, but the method of determining the price, a permissible option. Will you be able to figure out that method? If so, will you take the time? Other than accountants and lawyers, very few people actually do take the time to figure out this sort of thing in their contracts.

Regulation M, however, does require that such information be written clearly and, already, this has resulted in a greater clarity of language in some lease contracts. But clarity is not easy to define, and you can be sure that lessors will be seeking the edge, that gray area where clarity and obfuscation merge.

And when considering clarity as defined by law, keep in mind that federal tax code requires that the tax laws be written clearly.

LEASING BASICS

In order to effectively negotiate a lease, it is essential that you become thoroughly familiar with every facet of leases—their components, jargon, and how they operate. The first step is to know the different types of leases.

TYPES OF LEASES

In a threatening world, it's good to know that a kind of lease that was once common—and dangerous to the health of your bank account—has all but disappeared: the open-end lease.

Open-End Leases

Open-end leases have a feature that, from your point of view, can be highly unpleasant. Namely, you are responsible for insuring that the lessor makes the money he wants to make on the deal. In other words, you are responsible for the residual value of the car being equal to the estimate made when you leased it.

That value is determined by the market—even if you simply return the car to the lessor. When the lease expires, the residual value estimated *x* number of years ago is compared to what that model is going for at the current fair market price.

But what does that mean? Clean? Average? Rough? Wholesale? Retail? If retail, at what degree of discount? Who decides?

As you can see, there's many a catch in an open-end lease. And, once, many people got caught. Someone would bring back a car. A guy at the dealership or lease store would look at it. Then he'd look at some charts. Then he'd hold out his hand and ask for money. Lots of it. Now, open-end leases are comparatively rare. But some banks and a few lease stores still offer them. So watch out. Unless you're an expert, and your circumstances are unusual, avoid any lease that makes you responsible for the lessor's recoupment of any part of the residual value when the lease expires.

Closed-End Leases (with an option to buy)

The leases you encounter will probably be closed-ended, but check to be sure. With a closed-end lease, you owe nothing at the end of the lease if you return the car. (Except, perhaps, for that cracked windshield you thought the dealer might pay for. He won't.) If the lease contains an end-of-term purchase option, permitting you to buy the car, the purchase price will probably be specified. Specified though it is, it may not be the "actual" price required by the lender, so it may be negotiable.

Disposition Fees

Disposition fees, purportedly to cover the cost of disposing of the car, create the exception to the rule that you owe nothing at the end of a closed-end lease. Some banks charge disposition fees whenever you return the car, and they can be as high as $400. If your potential lessor charges one, check the total of the monthly payments against the same total on deals without the fee, offered by other lenders. And tell your salesperson what you are doing and why. Make sure the payment total plus the disposition fee is not significantly higher than the total payout on the other deals. If it is, reject the deal with the disposition fee. And tell your salesperson why.

The Lease-End Purchase Option

Some lessors offer closed-end leases that automatically include a lease-end purchase option. Others make it a feature you must choose and, in some cases, pay for. Still others do not offer it at all. The purchase option is a good thing if the price is right. The car may be the best you've ever had. Or it may have "a big book" (have held its value unusually well and be worth a lot of money) enabling you to profit from buying and reselling it.

When comparing lease deals, check to see if the purchase option is there. If there's a charge for it, compare the cost with and without it, then compare the cost with it to other leases that include it automatically. Most major automakers' credit companies' leases include purchase options at no charge. Usually, you will find one of two options:

   a. Price preset at the official residual value and written into the contract. Although preset, this figure may still be negotiable.

   b. Price not set, but to be determined later by "fair market value." This can mean anything, so no one, least of all you, can know in advance what the price will be.

Fair market price is used in leases offered by some banks and finance companies. You may safely assume that the "fair market value" discovered at the end of the lease will not favor you. The price will be set toward the high retail end of a price spectrum that begins at wholesale, so you may be able to negotiate it down.

Does a preset lease-end purchase price necessarily mean a good deal? No. You want it to be a good deal, of course, and you also want it to be accurate, that is, to include no unstated profit for the middleman (dealer or lease store). For, even if you do not buy the car at the end of the lease, this buyout or purchase price will be your "nut"; it will determine whether or not you can make any money by selling the car.

Getting a lease-end purchase price that is both accurate and a decent deal may not be easy, but it sure is worth a try. Later, in chapter 9, we'll talk about how to go about trying.

UNITS OF MONEY: THE COMPONENTS OF A LEASE

As we've mentioned, when you lease, you buy a fraction of a car's life. That fraction must therefore be converted into an amount of money. To do that, you begin with the amount that represents the car's full life value.

Selling Price

When the dealer figures out your lease payment he bases it on a retail price. That price can be the full sticker price of the car ("full pop"), it can be more than the sticker price, or it can be a discounted price, as low as a hundred or two over dealer cost. There is no one set lease price or lease payment. On a car that retails for (has a sticker price of) $20,000, the fraction of value you use up can be a fraction of $20,000, or a fraction of a discounted price of, say, $18,500. Your lease payment may be based on a price that is a good deal for you or a good deal for the dealer. It is a matter of negotiation.

So the purchase price upon which your lease payment is based is the first important amount, or unit, of money in a lease deal. It is also known as the sell price, selling price, or deal price.

Manufacturer's Suggested Retail Price (MSRP)

The next important unit is the Manufacturer's Suggested Retail Price (MSRP) before deductions for options package discounts. "Options package" or "options group" discounts are factory discounts off the total price of a preselected group of options. You don't pick them: the options in the group are determined by the manufacturer. Some packages contain only a few options, the total price of which is discounted only $50 to $100. And some contain ten or more, with a discounted price many hundreds of dollars lower than the total retail price of all the options in the group.

In this book we will use MSRP not to mean sticker or list price, but to mean the manufacturer's suggested price *before* the package discount is subtracted. Sticker price or list price (also sometimes called the MSRP on the window sticker) will mean the car's price after the discount is deducted. It is important to distinguish these two prices because the MSRP before the discount is the amount most lenders use to calculate the car's residual value.

Residual Value

Next, then, is residual value. Ford calls it lease-end value. Others call it the end-of-term value. Whatever it's called, this is what the lessor or lender thinks the car will be worth when the lease expires. It is calculated as a percentage of MSRP before manufacturer's discounts. It differs from car to car and, for most cars with most lenders, it goes down every one or two months following the month of the car's introduction. It, too, is used to calculate your payment, and the larger it is, the lower your payment will be, because basically your payment is based on the difference between the price of the car and what it will be worth at the end of the lease term.

Capitalized Cost, Acquisition Cost, or Net Agreed Value

This is the amount from which the residual value is subtracted to find one of the sums you'll pay off. It's called capitalized cost (abbreviated as "cap" cost), acquisition cost, net agreed value, or a number of other things. It is equal to the selling price plus any fees or additional purchases and minus any cash or trade equity you put down.

Depreciation

This is the amount your payment pays off before interest or lease charges. In a nutshell, it equals capitalized cost minus residual value. Thus it represents the estimated portion of the car's value that you will use during the lease. A few lenders use other terms, but "depreciation" is the most widely used.

Interest or Lease Charges

Then there's interest. Some folks will tell you that you pay no interest on a lease. Borrow money and pay no interest? Fat chance. The thing is, lease interest is calculated differently than the interest on installment purchase loans. And so it often goes by different names, like interest, the lease rate, lease interest, and lease charges. The quick method of calculating lease interest is to multiply the balance subject to lease charges (cap cost plus residual value) by the money factor (one half the monthly interest rate, expressed as a decimal). Later, we will discuss the calculation of lease interest in much more detail.

Lease-End Buyout (or Payoff) or End-of-Term Purchase Price

The lease-end buyout is the amount, written into the contract, that you agree to pay if you wish to buy the car at the end of the lease. It may be equal to the stated residual value. It may be that fraction of the car's purchase price which you have not paid off, which could be different from the residual value. Or it may be some other figure. What figure? A figure you never discover.

If the lease-end buyout equals the residual value, the amount is usually an estimated future high retail price, a price the lessor hopes the car will bring on the market.

In addition, there may be another, lower, unmentioned buyout, normally equal to estimated future wholesale value of the car. This lower buyout is the amount the lessor must get in order to make an acceptable return on its investment.

Early Buyout

Finally, if you want to buy, or buy and resell the car before your lease is up, there is the early buyout, or lease payoff during the term of the lease. If you buy out the lease early, you will pay off what the lessor spent to buy the car and the interest that has accumulated up to that point. Therefore, you should not be charged a prepayment penalty. Normally, however, you are. It's called an early termination penalty and most banks charge one. Chrysler Credit charges one. GMAC used to, but now does not. Ford charges one, but, in my experience, the dealer can usually persuade the company to forgo it.

Obviously, both early buyouts and lease-end payoffs have a few little wrinkles that can be costly. Not so obvious is the fact that you may never know what either of them really is. The "true" lease-end purchase price can differ from the one specified in the contract. And there is no specified price for early buyouts. Someone knows what they are, of course. But depending on who you lease from, some of the people who know will refuse to tell you. And others who know may try to mislead you. More about this in chapter 9, but for now, the possibility of early lease terminations leads to another question.

How Long Will the Romance Last—Or, Is There a Best Length of Lease Term?

Leases commonly run two, three, four, and five years. No particular term is best. A two-year lease might be just what you need or a five-year lease might be best.

In the late eighties and early nineties, four- and five-year leases were the most common. Now, in the late nineties, two- and three-year leases are more common, due solely to manufacturers' subsidies. I have a hunch that four- and five-year leases may make a comeback, if the price of cars continues to rise faster than inflation, and much faster than the average wage.

But right now, manufacturers want short leases. So salespeople will tell you four or five years is too long, because the car will go out of warranty. While it is true that the typical 3-year/36,000-mile bumper-to-bumper warranty will expire, what they don't tell you is that the manufacturer's powertrain warranty covers the car for five years or 60,000 miles. So if you lease for four years at 15,000 miles per year, you will be covered for the most areas most expensive to repair (engine, transmission or transaxle, and front-wheel-drive components) during the entire term.

The principles are the same no matter what the term. For you, the determining factors will be:

· Factory subsidies. These can make a two-year lease payment lower than a three-year payment, a three-year lower than a four-year.
· Your expectations. Do you anticipate a rise in income after two, three, four, or five years? Or will greater financial burdens (house, children, etc.) cancel out any increase or even lower your disposable income? Are you

the type who wants a new car every two years? Will you be in a position to afford the "car of your dreams" in a few years and will you want to upgrade?

· Warranty coverage. Consider the length and breadth of warranty coverage in relation to the number of miles you will drive.

Below are a few other things to think about and cost comparisons for the common lease terms.

Factory-subsidized Short-term Leases

If you are interested in a short-term lease (24 to 39 months) check to see if the manufacturer's credit arm is offering bargain rates.

As the price of new cars continues to climb, manufacturers are offering more super deals on two-year leases in order to accelerate the trading cycle and sell more cars. By "super," I mean lease rates of 2% to 4%, instead of the usual 7% to 10%. You may have to ask about this. In some areas of the country, some dealers, believing few customers want very short leases, will not spend the money to advertise short-term bargains, unless the manufacturer copays for the ads. If, however, a subsidized lease is available, you can save $50 or more per month.

As of this writing, you are not likely to find subsidized four- and five-year leases. Generally speaking, the shorter the term and the higher the price, the greater the likelihood of subsidies. But, as mentioned, that may change over the next couple of years.

Subsidizing Methods

There are three methods of subsidizing leases: buying down interest rates (charging less than the going market rate also used on purchases); inflating residual values; and forcing (or subsidizing) dealers to give heavy discounts.

Sometimes these subsidies provide you with a very good deal indeed. But there are some things you should consider carefully.

First, manufacturers promote short-term leases heavily with slogans like "Drive a New Car Every Two Years!" But bear in mind that in two or three years your next lease payment will probably be 10% to 12% higher—or maybe more because of the rise in car prices. Can you afford this increase in two years? Do you really want to get rid of your car and get another one after only two years? Getting a car can be a hassle and two years goes by rapidly.

Also, consider the size of the down payment. Is the deal really a bargain or are you making up for that low payment by putting down a hefty chunk of cash?

A Good Subsidy Deal

Here's an example of a good subsidy deal. Nissan has been leasing its Maxima, with automatic transmission and lots of goodies, listing for about $22,800, for 36 to 39 months, no money down, at $299.90 per month before taxes. Mileage allowance is 45,000 total, or 15,000 per year. The stated residual value was 54%. Depending on the size of the discount off list price (a good deal larger than the one in our examples below) and on the actual residual value, the lease or interest rate comes to between 2.2% and 2.5%.

That's a good deal, but you have to be alert to get it. Nissan also offers the same car and same payment with $1,000 down and Nissan dealers sometimes offer the same car and the same payment with $1,500 down. The deal with $1,000 down is not a bad one, but nowhere near as sweet as with zero down. (See appendix C for how to gauge the value of an advertised lease deal.)

Comparing Payments for Different Lease Terms

To give you an idea of monthly payment cost in relation to lease term, here are some examples. These payments are calculated using residual values from residual value charts published near the beginning of the model year. That's when residuals are highest and lease payments lowest. However, the charts used are fairly conservative: not the best deal you can get. The same is true of the discounts and the interest rates.

The first price in each example is the MSRP. The "selling price" is the actual price after a negotiated discount.

The payments are before taxes and do not include bank or lessor acquisition fees. And the payments are based on mileage allowances of 15,000 per year.

Note: A few years ago, leases allowing 15,000 miles per year were by far the most common. Now, however, mileage allowances are all over the map. Newspaper ads feature leases with allowances from 7,500 to 15,000. So think carefully about how many miles you drive per year and check the small print.

TWO-YEAR PAYMENT, NOTHING DOWN:
$15,000 car (selling price $14,100), 47% residual: $374.12
$20,000 car (selling price $18,600), 49% residual: $473.17
$30,000 car (selling price $28,200), 51% residual: $702.80

SUBSIDIZED TWO-YEAR PAYMENT, NOTHING DOWN:
$15,000 car, 2.75% rate: $317.99
$20,000 car, 2.75% rate: $399.21
$30,000 car, 2.75% rate: $587.35
$30,000 car, 60% residual, 2.75% rate: $477.94
$30,000 car, 60% residual, 3.00% rate: $482.75

(Notice that if we take the last item at $482.75 and subtract the $83 per month saved by a $2,000 down payment, we find that 24-month, $399 payment you often see advertised for cars in the $30,000 range—with, of course, $2,000 down.)

THREE-YEAR PAYMENT, NOTHING DOWN:
$15,000 car, 40% residual: $301.38
$20,000 car, 42% residual: $384.58
$30,000 car, 45% residual: $566.79
$30,000 car, 52% residual: $514.25

SUBSIDIZED THREE-YEAR PAYMENT, NOTHING DOWN:
$15,000 car at 2.75% rate: $248.03
$20,000 car at 2.75% rate: $314.27
$30,000 car at 2.75% rate: $456.12
$30,000 car, 52% residual, 2.75% rate: $400.19

Four-Year Leases

Four years represents a basic compromise between lowness of payment, length of warranty coverage, and reliability of vehicle. Subsidies are rare with four-year terms; when they do exist, the factory typically knocks about two percentage points off the going lease rate. However, as mentioned, expect to see more four-year lease deals in the future.

FOUR-YEAR PAYMENT, NOTHING DOWN:
$15,000 car, 33% residual: $263.01
$20,000 car, 35% residual: $337.67
$30,000 car, 39% residual: $507.33

(Notice that the subsidized three-year payment is substantially lower than the unsubsidized four-year payment.)

Five-Year Leases

Advantage: low payment. Disadvantage: possible unreliability and high maintenance costs during the fifth year. Another possible disadvantage is that you may be tired of the car or your needs may change.

FIVE-YEAR PAYMENT, NOTHING DOWN:
$15,000 car, 28% residual: $234.54
$20,000 car, 30% residual: $302.24
$30,000 car, 34% residual: $453.79

66-Month Leases

These have been available nationwide for some time for expensive vehicles, but for low- and medium-priced vehicles they are relatively new, especially in the East. They have the same advantages and disadvantages as five-year leases, only more so. If you are tempted by a 66-month lease, check it carefully. Some of them advertise astoundingly low payments, but give you astoundingly low mileage allowances. One, for example, allows 41,250 total miles. Over 66 months, that's 7,500 miles a year: only half that included with the payments quoted above. Exceeding the allowance brings a charge of ten to fifteen cents per mile. This could lead to a highly unpleasant hit to your bank account.

LEASING VS. BUYING

WILL LEASING COST MORE IN THE LONG RUN?

It may, or it may not. It's hard to tell, because the long-term costs of leasing versus those of buying depend on too many variables for there to be any hard and fast rule. Some of those variables are: the kind of car you lease or buy, when you do the deal, whether or not you buy add-ons like rust-proofing and extended warranties (usually unnecessary with a lease), whether or not the manufacturer is offering subsidized buy rates or subsidized leases, and the condition of the car you bought when you try to sell it.

The condition of the car can be a real kick in the head. Although most people think their cars are wonderful, most cars are average and not so hot.

In terms of pure dollars and cents, the way to save money in the long run is to buy the car, put very few miles on it, keep it in perfect shape, and then sell it to yourself for something close to a dealer's retail price. But dollars and cents are never pure.

First there are the benefits I mentioned earlier: more available cash or credit, less money down, and driving a nicer car with lower payments. These are real, solid benefits, and they are worth money. The amount varies, of course, from person to person. Consider them in light of your own circumstances.

Second, selling a car involves work. Keeping a car in good shape also involves time and effort, and the amount could be considerable. If you are a person who normally trades in your old car, selling a car may well involve more work than you really want to do.

Remember, too, that although sellers tend to overlook wear and tear on their own cars, prospective buyers tend to notice it.

LONG-TERM COST COMPARISONS

Let's take a couple of cars for examples and see how to work out the difference in long-term cost between a buy and a lease. We'll compare a low-priced car, a mid-priced car, and an expensive model.

Note: To calculate buy payments, get a loan payment book that includes tables for short-term (two-to-six-year) loans. Look at the cost of a $1,000 loan at the appropriate percentage rate and term your bank or dealer is offering. Then put a decimal point and a zero in front of that number and round it off to five digits. Now you have the factor for that term and interest rate.

A factor is a number that, when multiplied against a sum of money, will tell you what the monthly payment is for a particular interest rate and loan term.

For example, the payment on $1,000 borrowed for four years at 9.5% interest is $25.12. Thus, the forty-eight-month factor for 9.5% is .02512. To calculate your payment, multiply the amount you are borrowing by the factor. If you borrowed $10,000, multiply by .02512 = $251.20.

Calculating lease payments is a whole other story, covered in greater detail beginning on page 99. For now, I'll just supply them for the examples below.

Low-Priced Car

The MSRP on our Ford Escort is $13,320, minus an $870 options package discount for a final sticker price of $12,450. It's a four-door automatic, with air conditioning, cloth seats, power steering, AM/FM stereo/cassette, power mirrors, light group, clearcoat paint, body side moldings, and a few other little niceties. We'll assume that you can buy or lease the car for a price of $11,800, including the $10 to $30 the dealer charges for the inspection fee, titling fee, or other minor additional charges.

How big a discount is that $650? After the Ford "options package discount" (for selecting a bunch of options in a group) of $870, the markup on the car would be about $995. The dealer, however, will "pack" the car with at least $100. The "pack" is an amount, usually $100 to $200, that the owner adds to the invoice cost for "overhead."

As you would expect, the owner and his managers regard the pack as truly part of a car's cost, so the markup shrinks. Our Escort is left with $895 or so "effective" or "after-pack" markup. A $650 discount thus leaves a profit of $245, minus the inspection fee and so on, say $15, giving us a deal at $230 over dealer cost ("$230 over"). This is not the best possible deal, perhaps, but it's a good one.

Sales tax varies from place to place; I'll use 7% here. At 7%, tax on the buy at $11,800 will be $826. Let's assume we put no money down and finance the whole shot: $12,626.

At the moment I write, banks and dealers are quoting interest rates of 9% to 10% for a buy and 8% for a lease. I'll use 9.25% as the buy rate and 8.5% as the lease rate. (Unless a manufacturer is offering lower than market rates, nominal lease rates usually run a point to a point and a half below the buy rate. So I'm stacking the deck slightly in favor of the buy.)

If you buy the car, financing $12,626 for four years at 9.25%, your payment will be about $315.70 a month.

If you lease the car early in the model year for 48 months at 8.5% with an $11,800 sell price, and $300 added on for a bank fee, your payment on a relatively standard lease deal will be $219.29 plus a 7% tax per payment of $15.35. Your total monthly payment would be $234.64. The lease would allow 15,000 miles per year, with an 11-cents-per-mile penalty for excess miles.

After forty-eight buy payments you'd put out $15,153.60. After forty-eight lease payments you'd put out $11,262.72. The lease would save you a total of $3,890.88, or $81.06 each month.

Trading In

If you buy the car, pay off the loan, then sell the car or trade it in, what will it be worth? Nobody knows. Judging by today's prices, somewhere between $3,500 and $5,500. If you trade it in, you'll probably get between $3,200 and $4,300. The "trade allowance" your salesperson tells you about may be higher than the car's cash value, but the overage will consist of what are called "show dollars": the discount off the retail price of the new car.

If you traded in, then, and got $3,200 for the Escort, your net expense to buy would be $11,953. Leasing would save you $691. If the Escort were in good shape, and you got $4,500 for it, buying would save you around $600.

Selling the Car

But suppose you sell the car yourself? Won't you get a lot more? You'll get more, but perhaps not as much as you think.

You may see Escorts like yours advertised by dealers for close to $6,000. But they've been marked up close to $2,000, and the markup includes additional costs, such as overhead, inspection, repair and clean-up work, the price of the used car warranty, and sales commissions. It also includes discountable money.

Remember, dealers set prices based on the assumption that everybody demands a discount. If a customer walks through the door and smiles, the store will knock off three hundred dollars. If a customer walks through the door and frowns and then bargains hard, the store will knock off eight hundred to a thousand.

The additional costs the dealer's price must cover include: the state mandated Lemon Law warranty (if the state mandates one), the replacement of bald tires, a state inspection, a lube and oil change, a fill-up of the antifreeze and squirter fluid, replacement or reattachment of body side moldings, replacement of missing knobs and levers, a steam cleaning of the engine, an interior vacuuming and shampoo, a wash and wax, etc.

Additional Considerations

Here are some of the variables that must be taken into consideration when estimating what your car will be worth, and comparing costs of leasing vs. buying:

- The car's condition.
- Mileage.
- Availability of that model in your area.
- Demand for that model in your area.
- The model's repair/reliability record.
- The price of gasoline (cheap gas lowers the value of small cars, and vice versa).
- Whether or not you earn interest on your monthly lease savings. (If you deposited your $80-a-month savings on the Escort lease, you would earn $250 to $350 in interest.)
- Selling costs, if you sell the car yourself (for the tune-up and cleanup, plus the newspaper ad, plus $10 to $40 a week to keep the car registered and insured). Selling costs could consume any savings realized by buying and reselling. Don't forget them.
- Whether the lease has a purchase option, and if so, the price. If you had negotiated a low purchase option price ($4,200 to $4,500) and could sell the Escort yourself for $5,500, you would pocket the profit. Minus selling costs, of course.
- And, finally, if your car is in good shape, whether or not you've spent a lot of money on maintenance to keep it in good shape.

Another possibility to consider is that your four-year-old Escort with 59,000 miles on it could be a little ratty worth only $2,900.

Buy		Lease	
Total payments	$15,153	Total payments	$11,262
Trade in for	−$2,900	They clip your security deposit for dings	+$250
Total cost	$12,253	Total cost	$11,512

In this case—even if you had to give up a chunk of your security deposit—leasing would save you money.

Exceptions

It may occur to you that extremely low purchase loan rates provided by the manufacturer will change long-term cost outcomes. However, at times when extremely low purchase finance rates are being offered, extremely low lease rates are usually being offered, too.

Midpriced Car

For the sake of a peculiar kind of nostalgia, let's do a Chevrolet Monte Carlo, a nineties revival of an eighties classic. It will have an automatic transmission, air conditioning, tilt steering wheel, and power steering, brakes, locks, and windows, and let's say the MSRP is $18,345. Dealer cost with interest, advertising charges, and pack added would be about $17,100.

I'm not choosing the Monte solely for nostalgia's sake. The price and the less-than-super residual value make it representative of a whole bunch of cars in that price range, cars by Chrysler, GM, and Ford and a few of the less stellar Asian brands.

At the moment of this writing, GM is offering cash back on a whole slew of cars, with the Monte Carlo qualifying for a nice, round $1,000. We'll hand that over to the dealer as a down payment—or "capitalized cost reduction." And then let's assume we negotiate a price of $400 over cost, leaving us with a lease capitalized cost, or a buy price after $1,000 cash down, of $16,500.

On a buy, sales tax is paid up front, so we'll add 7% for the tax and come to $17,655. Again, we will take no cash out of pocket, so we'll finance the whole thing. The payments for a 48-month loan of $17,655 at 9.25% will be about $441.44 a month.

I say "about" to introduce you to the fact that, on occasion, a payment based on the rate charts used at a car store will be $0.50 to $1.00 higher than the payment found in a mortgage payment book for the same amount borrowed at the same interest rate. Some dealership loan charts sweeten the juice. Ours did. At $441.44 a month, you will pay $21,189.12 over four years.

Leasing the Monte Carlo for four years—based on the $16,500 price and a residual value reached by averaging three different charts—will cost $296.00 per month. Add 7% tax, and the monthly payment becomes $316.72. Multiply that by 48 for a total outlay of 15,202.56.

Monthly cash savings on the lease will be $124.72, or $5,986.56 over the four years. Interestingly enough, your savings will be a bit more than the car's wholesale value if it's average. Although pricing four-year-old Monte Carlos is a bit of a guessing game at this point, we can make a fairly educated estimate that wholesale on an average four-year-old Monte, with fairly basic equipment like our example, will be $5,700 to $6,000.

If you buy the car and trade it in, that's what you'll get. So if you trade in, leasing and buying will cost you about the same in the long term.

What if you factor in interest earnings on your savings of

$124 a month? With a money market account earning 4.5%, your $124 monthly deposits will earn you about $553 over the four years. With a CD earning 6%, your interest earnings would be about $740.

So if you deposit your lease savings, total savings rises to $6,540 or $6,730 depending on the interest earned. If you bought the car instead, and then traded it in, leasing would save you $500 to $700. But what if you sell the car yourself? How much could you expect? If your car were average, you could expect to recover $6,000 to $6,800, depending where it fell in the spectrum of average. If you bought and then resold the car for a price in that range, the long-term costs of buying and leasing would be about equal.

Buy		**Lease**	
Total buy payments	$21,189	Total lease payments	$15,202
Less sale price	−$6,800	Less interest earned	−$553
Net expense	$14,389	Net expense	$14,649
(Plus selling costs: ads, tune-up, repairs, insurance)	+150	(Less interest at 6%)	−$187
Net expense	$14,539	Net expense	$14,462
(Less sale price at $7,000)	−$200		
Net expense	$14,339		

You may think that a four-year-old car in this class will bring more than $7,000. Maybe it will. And maybe it won't. Remember, if it's average it will have, say, 57,000 miles on it, and with those miles will come a few dings. The four-year residual values we averaged out ranged from 34% to 39%, resulting in residual value amounts of $6,237 to $7,154.

These are retail prices. They would serve as your official lease-end buyout prices, unless you negotiated lower ones. In other words, these are prices that the respective lenders consider to be fairly fat. Now, I am not subtracting interest lost on your lease security deposit, or taxes from your interest earnings. Neither am I subtracting the loss of value due to inflation from the money you make selling the Monte Carlo. These will tend to cancel each other out; additionally, selling costs could be considerably higher than $150. In some areas, it could cost up to $40 a week just to keep the car insured while you're selling it. So, as before, individual circumstances vary so much that no absolute pronouncements are possible. In the cases we've been discussing, if you wanted or needed the monthly savings offered by leasing, you could get them without sacrificing much, if anything, in long-term costs.

On the other hand, your Monte might be extra clean with very low miles, worth $8,000. Should this be the case, you could sell the car, pay off the lease, and take the overage.

Another possibility, and a real one: your Monte may be worth only $5,400. If you bought and resold, you'd lose money.

Finally, if you bought and then traded in, you very probably could do no better than break even when compared to the lease.

More Expensive Car

Let's look at a subsidized lease versus a subsidized buy. Nissan once offered a deal: 5.9% financing to buy a Maxima

GXE, or $300 a month for a 39-month lease, both with nothing down. The lease offered 15,000 miles per year.

Let's say the car's cost is $21,304 and its price is $23,739. We'll do a hell of a deal and buy it for $21,600. Add 7% tax and we have $23,112.

If we buy, our monthly payment on a 39-month loan would be $652.70. After 39 payments, we will have spent $25,455. Assuming we sell it for $12,800 (and it cost us nothing to sell it!) we spent a total of $12,655.

Now for the lease. Adding tax brings our $300 payment to $321. This monthly payment times 39 equals $12,519.

We saved $136 by leasing. If you trade the car in, you'll probably be paid $11,000 to $12,000, so the dealer can advertise it at $14,000 to $15,000, then discount it $1,000 and still make a nice buck.

Admittedly, this Nissan lease is an extraordinary deal. But even if we had lost $500 by leasing, we would have had $300 extra dollars in our pocket every month for 39 months.

Rules of Thumb

You're probably getting the picture. Circumstances — like car care habits, mileage driven, and the value of used cars — vary too greatly for there to be any ironclad rules. Still, there are some rules of thumb you can consider to help you make an informed decision on whether to lease or buy a car.

If you drive an average number of miles, and take average care of your car, the long-term costs of a buy and a lease on a new, low-priced car are pretty much the same. As long as you lease right, this would be true even compared to you selling the car yourself and getting a decent but not great price for it. The more "average" your car is, the more likely you are to save by leasing. If you would otherwise trade your car in, you will probably save by leasing.

If you drive few miles and keep your car in excellent shape, you will probably save by buying and reselling. If you drive very few miles, you have little reason to lease, because you would be paying for miles you don't use.

However, if you drive few miles, say, 7,000 miles a year, and then trade your car in, be careful to base your cost comparisons on a low-mileage lease, one allowing from 7,500 to 10,000 miles a year. Because if you trade your car in, you will be paid wholesale, or "actual cash value," and a low-mileage lease may save you money.

When you do your cost comparison, try to be objective about your car care habits and realistic about how you dispose of cars. Many people take good care of a car for the first year or so, then slack off. And many people say to themselves, "Oh, I'll sell it for a real good price," then end up trading it in.

At this point, many people say: "But I won't have anything after four years." One thing you won't have is the time and work spent cleaning up and selling your car. With a little bad luck, that time and work can be a major pain in the neck.

One thing you will have is $50 to $150 a month (depending on the cost of the car and the length of the lease) and what that money will earn in interest.

Even if you spend the money and it earns zip, you will not have precisely "nothing." You may have gained years of pleasure from the new computer, VCR, washer and dryer, or beer, pretzels, and sporting events you spent the money on.

Lease and Loan Terms

Does the length of a lease or buy affect the cost comparison? What about buying vs. leasing with two-, three-, and five-year terms? A host of factors come into play and the results are pretty much the same no matter what the term. You have to consider long-term cost comparisons in terms of specific vehicles and your specific habits and circumstances. Typically, the longer the term, the greater the chance for your car to be in "average" condition, so the more likely the lease is to save you money.

Buying on a five-year loan is probably not the best way to go. If the lowest possible payment is your goal, a five-year lease will provide them. If you are flexible as to payments, those of a four-year lease tend to be a little less than those of a five-year buy. And you are out of the car after four years — without having to worry about paying off the balance on the loan. Neither do you have to keep paying through that fifth year for a car that may have become a little less than wonderful. Again: if you drive very few miles and keep your car in excellent shape, leasing loses some of its allure. Lease a car that you'll drive five or six thousand miles a year and you will pay for mileage that you do not use.

Note: Your lender may charge lease or buy rates different from those above. Or rates may have changed nationwide. You cannot use these figures except as examples with which to practice and to understand how to make the comparison.

So, too, with the values of the used cars. Fact: people in different parts of the country like different kinds of cars. You may live in a market where everybody loves the car I'm discussing, thus inflating its price. Or where nobody would be caught dead in that particular car, drastically reducing its price. You must discover the details that pertain to your locality.

CASH DOWN TO LOWER BUY PAYMENTS

One frequently sees advice to the effect that you should put as much cash down on a car as you can afford. Then buy it by taking the shortest loan whose payments you can afford. By doing so, you are supposed to save money on interest charges.

My feeling is that if you have tons of money, maybe you should do this. However, if you don't have tons of money, you probably shouldn't.

First, answer a question: where will the cash down come from? If it will come from a bank or mutual fund, it should be earning interest for you. The next question is, will your savings in unpaid interest for the car loan be more than your earned interest on the cash left sitting in the bank? Here's how to figure it out.

We'll compare a buy with cash down to one with nothing down, then a buy with cash down to a lease with nothing down. Let's use the Escort, on which we were financing $12,626. We'll assume you're not too happy with that $315.70 monthly payment, so you decide to put down $2,000.

If you put down $2,000 and pay off $10,626 at 9.25% over four years, you'll pay $265.69 a month.

Total monthly payments with no cash down: $315.70 × 48 = $15,153.60

Total monthly payments with $2,000 down: $265.69 × 48 = $12,753.12

Savings: $15,153.60 − $12,753.12 = $2,400.48, or $2,400.

Or, an alternate way to do it: payment with $0 down minus payment with $2,000 down: $315.70 − $265.69 = $50.01. Difference times number of months equals savings: $50.01 × 48 = $2,400.48

With $2,000 down, you pay, over the life of the loan, $2,400 less. In other words, putting down $2,000 saved you $400 in interest.

On the other hand, if that $2,000 sits in a money market account at 4.75% compounded monthly for four years, it will earn about $408. You'll be $8 ahead of the game. And, more importantly, you'll have the $2,000 available should you happen to need it. If that $2,000 sits in a 6% CD compounded monthly for four years it will earn $541 in interest. You'll be $141 ahead of the game, and, again, the cash will be available for emergencies.

Your $2,000 earns more interest than it saves you simply because the amount you are earning interest on increases with compounding. To find out how much interest your proposed down payment will earn, just call a local bank. Pick one that pays interest compounded monthly. Ask how much you'll have after four years if you deposit that amount in its 48-month CD.

Here's the buy with $2,000 down compared to the lease with nothing down:

4-Year Buy, $2,000 Down		4-Year Lease, $0 Down	
Monthly payment	$265.69	Monthly payment	$234.64
48-month lease	×48		×48
Total	$12,753.12	Total	$11,262.72
Plus down payment	+$2,000.00	Less 6% interest on the $2,000 kept in a CD	−$541.00
Total	$14,753.12		
Less resale	−$4,000.00		
Net expense	$10,753.12	Net expense	$10,721.72

Again, you may be taxed on your interest earnings; you may spend a couple hundred to sell the car; the car may be worth either more or less than $4,000.

Figuring that these "maybes" will more or less cancel one another, the lease beats the buy. Total expense is about the same. But the lease leaves you in possession of the $2,000. Put it down on the car and it won't be there should you happen to need it in an emergency. A point I haven't mentioned is that there are investments that earn more than 4% to 6%. I use CDs and money market accounts as examples because they are insured and thus, barring disaster, safe. But you may find a higher-yielding investment that has the degree of safety you want.

Another Rule of Thumb

If you can invest at a rate reasonably close to the rate you will be charged for the car loan, it makes no sense to put money down. By close, I mean something like the spread we saw in our examples, where financing costs (interest you pay) were 9% to 10%, and earnings ran from 4.5% to 6% on safe and readily available investments. Thus, interest costs on financing were about three to five points higher than interest earnings on savings.

In terms of dollar amounts (whether you are considering a down payment on an installment loan, or a down payment on a lease): if investing the money will earn more in interest than putting it down on the car will save, or if those earnings equal the savings, or if earnings are only a little lower than savings, keep your cash.

Should You Buy for Cash?

Some folks dream of being able to pay cash for a car. But is it worth it? Let's compare the expense of buying for cash to the expense of leasing.

Suppose you buy an $18,000 car like a Chevy Lumina for $16,500 plus 7% tax, or $17,655 cash. You drive it for four years, then recoup $6,800 by selling it. How do you make out?

SCENARIO 1
$17,655 minus $6,800 equals $10,855 net expense.
$316.72 (lease payment) times 48 equals $15,202.

But instead of paying $17,655 for the car, you keep the money in a 6% CD and earn $4,775 in interest. So $15,202 minus $4,775 equals $10,427 net expense. Leasing saved you $428.

SCENARIO 2
You pay cash. Since you are not making lease payments you have an extra $316.72 available each month. You take it out of your income and put it in a money market account. After 48 months at 4.5%, you will have earned about $1,405 in interest. The $10,855 net buy expense minus $1,405 equals $9,450 net expense.

The difference between leasing's net expense in scenario 1 ($10,427) and this cash buy expense ($9,450) is $977. Buying for cash and investing the unpaid monthly payments saved you $977.

SCENARIO 3
Your car is a nice one, but you trade it in and get $6,000. Buying for cash and investing your unpaid monthly payments has saved you $77.

In assessing examples like these for your own purposes, you need to take into account your overall financial situation. For example, let's go back to scenario 2 and ask a question: Is it worth spending $977 over four years to retain control over $17,655? If you are sufficiently well off not to have any worries about emergencies for which you might need cash, no, it isn't worth it. If you are not that well off, it may indeed be worth it. Over four years, $977 amounts to about 1.5% per year.

One other thing you should be aware of: Cash will not get you a better deal at the car store. When you are financed through a bank, the bank pays cash to the dealer, and then collects from you. To the dealer, all deals are cash.

GETTING READY

By now, the big picture should be coming into view. But there are a few very important little things to learn—and a few decisions to make—before you go out and do the deal. For example:

- · How leasing might influence your choice of car
- · How to determine dealer cost
- · What is a good deal
- · When to make a lease deal
- · What to do with your present car
- · How to price your present car
- · Where to make the deal
- · How to calculate lease payments
- · How to understand advertisements

Which Car Is the Car for You?

The one you like. The car for you is the car that rings your bell.

Within reason, of course. Don't get a Corvette if you've got four kids and two dogs. And do look up the repair records in a consumer publication. Some manufacturers cut costs on some of their cars by cutting the weight, strength, and ruggedness of parts.

Then, if its breakdown record is more or less average, go with the car that steals your heart. Or the one that fits your family.

Leasing may affect your decision because two very similar cars can have very different payments. In the case of two cars priced approximately the same, the one with the higher residual value will cost you less per month. And therefore cost less overall, unless you buy it at the end of the term. In fact, if the residuals differ sufficiently, you can actually pay less for a more expensive car.

Take two low-priced cars, A and B. Car A has a little more equipment, because its manufacturer makes more stuff standard equipment and puts a little more in comparable packages. It retails for $14,900. Car B has a little less equipment and retails for $14,550. Let's say you can lease Car A based on a price of $13,450 and Car B for $13,100.

When I look up a major bank's 48-month residual values for the two cars, I find that A's residual value is 36% and B's is 33% (of "retail" or "sticker" price, because we'll assume no options package discount).

Assuming no package discounts, and a 10% lease rate, you pay (before tax) $246.86 per month for Car A, and $247.49 for Car B. Car A has bigger, wider tires, which provide better handling, a bigger engine, and a power driver

seat. You pay less and get more because the lender considers
A to have a higher residual value at the end of the lease.

If two or three different vehicles are equally suitable for
you — and you are not interested in buying out the lease —
compare the residual values. Go with the highest residual
and, everything else being equal, you will get a similar car
for less money — or maybe even more car for less money.

DETERMINING DEALER COST

Knowing these numbers may also help you decide between
cars, and they supply a vantage point that will help you
understand everything else. Dealer cost is like a mark on a
map to show where your house is when you move into a
strange neighborhood.

Using Cost and Price Books

Buy a copy of a new car price book, like *Edmund's New
Car Prices* or *Consumer Guide's New Car Price Guide*
(Publications International, Ltd., 3841 W. Oakton St., Sko-
kie, IL, 60076). Both are available at bookstores and drug-
stores and discount stores with big magazine racks. Or,
often, at the local library. Make sure the book is current.
Not too old — and not too new. Manufacturers raise car
prices when they introduce the new year's models, then usually raise them twice during the rest of the year: at the turn
of the calendar year, and in the spring. Obviously, you could
get a book that's out of date and does not cover a recent
price increase. But since the books come out before the
price bumps, you can also get a book that's not in date yet,
one that shows a price increase not yet in effect.

A solution is available from Consumer Union, publisher of Consumer Reports. For $10 to $15 per car, they'll mail you a cost and price list for any car(s) you specify, along with all available options (256 Washington St., Mt. Vernon, NY 10553). There are also on-line auto pricing services (e.g., http://www.carprice.com), which promise accurate dealer cost figures. As with the price books, take care to check their figures.

You may have to do a little work to adjust the numbers you find in these books. One thing to watch for is that some books clump together the freight charges for all cars in a section at the back of the book. If you forget to look up the freight back there, your cost and price numbers will be $300 to $500 lower than the actual amounts. Too picky? Well, I forgot to do it, then spent twenty minutes wondering why the lease payment I had just calculated was the best deal the world had ever seen. Freight charges are kept separate by both manufacturer and dealer but they are a nonnegotiable part of both the car's cost and its price. Turning to the back of the book isn't much work. You may have to do a bit more when adjusting both retail price and dealer cost figures.

Price

The difficulty with price occurs because of options package discounts (a number of options are grouped together, then tagged as a group with a discounted price). When you buy, package discounts mean little. But when you lease, they mean a lot because cars with them—"package cars," as they are called—have two retail prices, one before and one after the discount.

The price before the discount, which we're calling the MSRP, is the one used to calculate the car's residual value.

The second, which we're calling "sticker price" or "retail," is the retail price of the car as it sits on the lot.

The key to recognizing package cars of any make or model is those two prices on the window sticker. Look for them. The sticker will show the base price for the car, the freight charges, perhaps some options not in the package, then a bunch of options in a group identified with letters or numbers. Then everything will be added up: base, freight, other options, and the retail price of each option in the package. The sum will be the MSRP. From that number the package discount will be subtracted, and what's left will be the sticker price, or something like this:

FABUCAR SPUDBOMB ZZT

Base price		$17,000
Freight [sometimes at end]		$300
Pearly Glow paint		$200
Options group 69A		
	option 1	$400
	option 2	$200
	option 3	$200
	option 4	$200
	option 5	$200
Options total price		$1,200
MSRP		$18,700
Discount on Option Group 69A		−$600
MSRP after discount (sticker price)		$18,100

The problem is that some consumer cost and price books ignore the price prior to the package discounts. They treat the options package as an item that has a cost to the dealer — the sum of the dealer costs for the options — and a retail price to you, which corresponds *not* to the sum of the retail prices of the options but to the already discounted price for the package.

A book that uses the already discounted package price to arrive at the price of the car will ignore the MSRP and show only the car's sticker price, $18,100, rather than $18,700 in terms of our example. But this is the price after the package discount. If you use that price to calculate residual value, you'll end up with residual that is too low, making the lease payment too high. You could sell yourself a bad deal.

Check your book to see how it handles package discounts. If it doesn't handle them, make sure you do. Unfortunately, if the book mentions options packages but not discounts, you'll have to visit a car lot and look at the window sticker of the model you want to see if it's a package car.

Cost/Dealer Cost

Once you have the price, or, if the car comes with a package discount, two prices, you then need to know dealer cost.

The consumer cost and price books will provide you with the base cost of the car, the costs of all the options and/or packages, and the delivery or freight charges.

Now you have a little more work to do to reach the total cost, for the dealer will add finance charges and advertising fees to the costs just mentioned.

If the manufacturer is *floorplanning* (financing) the dealership, the finance charges will appear on the car's invoice. If a bank is financing the dealership, the finance charges will appear on the dealer's books. Typically, at today's interest rates (late 1997) finance charges add about one-half to three-quarters of one percent to the cost of the car.

Also part of dealer cost is the dealer contribution to the factory's advertising program, sometimes called the dealer advertising fee. (Some manufacturers are said not to charge these fees. Check for the car you want.) Estimate another half to three quarters of one percent to cover advertising. Some new car cost and price books investigate these fees, but some do not. If your book does not, add 1% to 1.25% to the cost to account for the dealers finance and advertising fees.

Dealer cost, interestingly enough, includes a sum the dealer doesn't pay. When the car is sold and the dealer pays the factory, 3 to 4 percent is subtracted and either held out of the payment or kicked back later. That's the "holdback": a part of the "cost" that the dealer does not pay the factory. Owners of dealerships regard the holdback as sacred: theirs by divine right. They don't pay their salespeople a commission on it and they don't dip into it in order to give you a better deal.

Finally, the last cost item is the dealer's "pack" mentioned in chapter 3: $100 to $200 is added to the cost for "overhead." The size of the pack depends on the intensity of the competition in the area. Neighboring dealers usually add similar amounts. But unless you know someone in the business, the only way to discover that amount is to ask your salesperson. Estimate $100 for low-priced cars (below $11,000) and $150 for others. During negotiation, ask. And the time to ask is when the salesperson is insisting that you pay more than you are offering.

Do not, however, expect the pack to be discounted. Even in the East Babbitt car shoppers' paradise, with nine almost contiguous Ford dealers tearing at each other's throats, we did not discount down into the pack.

Here's a list of cost items:

Base price for the model (make sure you've got the right
number of doors: four-door cars are usually more expensive)

Option #1

Option #2

Option . . . #n

Freight (also called destination and delivery)

Finance charges

Dealer advertising fee

Subtotal: These items add up to "invoice cost," sometimes
called "dead cost" in the trade

Dealer cost adds: the pack

And, sometimes, illegitimately: "dealer prep"

If your dealer claims extra cost for prep, complain. The
manufacturer includes dealer prep in the retail price of the
car. If the dealer tries to charge you for it, he's trying to
charge you twice. Go somewhere else.

Additional Charges

At the East Babbitt Ford store, we charged an inspection
fee, but this was limited to the state fee for the sticker. We
also charged a "titling fee" of $10. This was $3 to New York
for the title and $7 to the dealer for the paperwork.

Our extra charges were low, but we were held in check

by the intensity of the competition. If you live in an area where competition is mild, the local dealer may try to hit you for more of these little extras. Object, strenuously. The dealer doesn't need them to make money. Besides, if they give you a good deal, you're going to lease your next five cars from them, right? Of course you are. Make sure they know it.

Lease Store Cost

A lease store buys vehicles from dealerships. Some of them receive a discount known as the "fleet discount" or "fleet incentive."

The amount of the fleet discount varies from manufacturer to manufacturer and from model to model. Over the last few years, the trend has been for manufacturers to reduce or eliminate it. If it exists, it can range from $100 off invoice cost, to the amount of the finance charges off invoice cost, all the way up to $700 off cost plus a free option or two. Whatever it is, the dealer will tack on a pack of $100 to $200 and a markup of $75 to $100.

When you figure cost to a lease store, you'll have to call dealerships or a factory rep to discover the amount of the fleet discount on the model you want. Then add a $150 pack and $100 for dealer profit. This will provide you with a preliminary estimate of the lease store's cost.

Then, when talking to the store's salesperson, you'll need to ask some more questions. Ask about:

a. The amount of the fleet discount off standard dealer cost—to make sure the store gets it and, if it does, to see how much of it is being passed on to you.
b. The amount of the dealer's pack and profit.
c. The lease store's pack and profit.

Even if the store refuses to discuss its pack and profit, once you have cost from a cost book and the amount of the fleet discount you can reach a fairly accurate estimate of the lease store's cost. And from there, of course, you can calculate the store's profit.

Cost of Trucks, Minivans, and Sport Utility Vehicles

Sport utility vehicles are things like Explorers and Broncos, Blazers and S-10 Blazers, and Jeep Cherokees. Although called "trucks," their cost and price are handled like cars, likewise with pickup trucks, minivans, and vans. Edmund's and other car cost book publishers also put out truck price books. If you are going to lease a truck, get one of those books, and take the same care with the numbers as with the car books.

The way you cost out a truck and the way you do the deal are exactly the same as with a car. Cost structure is the same as a car's, i.e., base, options, freight, finance charges, advertising, pack, etc. And so is price structure, with options packages and package discounts. So, too, then, is the need to find out if the MSRP before discount is higher than the sticker price.

Finally, you do deals and calculate lease payments the same way you do with cars. If, however, you will use the truck commercially, the lender will deduct 5% to 10% from its residual value.

WHAT EXACTLY IS A GOOD DEAL?

How much profit should the dealer make from you? Here are some guidelines.

On an "inexpensive" car in the Escort class (or below), which retails for $11,000 (or less) to $14,000: $200 to $250.

On a retail price of $14,000 to $18,000: $250 to $400.

On a retail price of $17,000 to $22,000: $350 to $500.

On a retail price of $22,000 to $27,000: $500 to 700.

On trucks, same as above.

This tends to work out to cost, or cost plus pack, plus something between 1.5 to 3 percent. You may be able to do better than these numbers, and it's definitely worth a try. But it's not worth a whole lot of time and anxiety. If you do something like the above, you've done well.

With some expensive vehicles, however, things may be a little different. More expensive vehicles can bring you eyeball to eyeball with the problem of scarcity. And scarcity doesn't blink. If demand for the car you want exceeds supply, you are no longer looking at cost plus, you are looking at sticker or sticker plus.

You should still determine dealer cost and negotiate as strongly as possible. But your bargaining power will be greatly reduced by the people coming in behind you who want the same car you do.

A Good Deal on a Lease Payment

When leasing, you have something to consider besides price. Will you want to buy the car eventually, or not? Most people don't.

If you will want to buy it, then a good deal payment consists of a combination of two things: the lowest payment you can get, in conjunction with the lowest lease-end purchase price you can find attached to that payment.

Normally, reducing the one leads to increasing the other: thus the lower the payment, the higher the lease-end purchase price or payoff. But if you seriously believe you'll buy the car, you want to strike a balance that results in the lowest total amount out of your pocket.

On the other hand, if you don't care about buying, you'll be concerned mainly with the lowest possible monthly payment—which often results in the highest possible payoff. But the high payoff will concern you only when it's time to see if you have equity in the car. It's a trade-off: the lower your payment, the less likely you are to have equity at the end of the lease.

Shop lenders for whichever deal is better for you.

Whether at a car store or lease store, find out who finances its lease deals. Get all of its financing sources, not just the one it uses most often. A store of any size will have at least two lenders it habitually uses and from one to five others it sometimes uses. Ask. If you do not ask, this information will not be offered. The people at the store will put your lease through the lender who pays them the most. (Interest rates on both buys and leases include a commission to the selling dealer.)

Find out what residual values these lenders use. Some will be higher than others.

Get payment quotes based on the different programs.

Do not accept for an answer, "Let me be honest with you. They're all the same." They are not all the same. Just as different lenders have different home mortgage programs, they also have different auto leasing programs.

Be persistent. Don't be embarrassed to repeat yourself.

And don't say you *want* to know; say you *have* to know or *need* to know. I spoke to a salesperson about a $16,300 car and was quoted a no-money-down payment of $286 per month for 48 months with a $5,000 buyout. I had to ask three times before she told me of a another lender's program, offering $273 a month with a buyout of $6,000. If I did not buy the car at the end of the lease, the second program would save me $661.

WHEN TO LEASE

When should you do the deal? Do it as close as possible to the beginning of the model year, and do it at the end of the month.

Beginning of the Model Year

Unless you are certain that the lease rate will go down substantially under a special manufacturer's program, you will have a lower payment if you lease at the beginning of the model year. The car's price will be lower and its residual or lease-end value will be higher. The longer a car has been out, the older it is and the lower its residual value.

For example, in the beginning of the model year, the four-year residual value factor for an Escort will be 32 to 35 percent. By the end of the year it will have dropped by 4 or 5 percent. Even without a price increase, this will raise the payment eight or nine dollars a month. Over forty-eight months, that adds up to a nice piece of change.

Not only will the car's residual value go down, but its price will probably go up. Manufacturers customarily bump prices at the turn of the calendar year and in the spring. So if you wait for a nice day in June to visit the car stores, you may well pay a premium for that good weather.

The End of the Month

For the people in car stores, the end of the month is a time of frenzy. Everybody has monthly quotas. The salesperson has a quota, his or her manager has a quota, and the dealership has a quota. Often, the quotas are optimistic, so by the end of the month everybody's desperate. And even if the quotas are met, everybody is hungry for that extra deal, that extra buck, to make the month a little better.

Should You Wait to Lease a Leftover Car at the End of the Model Year?

Generally speaking (there are exceptions), no. In most cases, they're not the bargain they're cracked up to be. Except for cars with limited production runs or cars that are scarce for some other reason, everything is on sale all year long. Even the exceptions to this are soft exceptions.

Right after the new models are introduced, for example, the managers will use the excitement of newness to try for bigger grosses. For the first few weeks after the new cars hit the showroom floor, it will be harder to get a good deal.

But time marches on. When the end of that particular month rolls around, the boys and girls will be sitting there staring at their quotas. And pondering their paychecks. No matter how much money they've made, one more deal will make them more. And, lo and behold, it's sale time.

What can you save by waiting till the end of the year? The end of the "year" in car time is August, the month preceding introduction of most manufacturers' new lines. Unless the model has sold miserably, the price of a car on a lot in August will have risen to the zenith, while its residual will have sunk to its nadir. This combination can raise the 48-month lease payment on a $15,000 car by $25 a month or more. It is unlikely that year-end discounts — rarely larger than the Sunday sale discounts — will be large enough to offset so large an increase.

It is also unlikely that the factory's inventory clearance rebates will offset it. These rebates, to help dealers get rid of their leftovers, run 3 to 5 percent. They will be about the same as the factory's price increases during the year. You can see that if the rebates cancel the year's price increases, they merely return you to the original price on a car that still costs you more per month because of its lower residual value.

On top of that, these rebates (called dealer incentives) are normally paid to the dealer, not to you. You get a piece of them only if the dealer gives it to you, and he will be generous only if stuck with too many unsold cars. Otherwise, the price will be cost plus pack, plus as much as he can get—just as it was during the year.

Therefore, a month or two after a new car hits the showroom floor, its price should be within $200 or $300 of the best deal you can get on a leftover. The higher residual value will compensate for the difference, so you may as well drive the car while it's depreciating and thus benefit from use value.

There's an old saying in the car business: "There's an ass for every seat." Unless the store is choked with inventory, the dealer will wait for the asses to find the seats rather than discount meaningfully (to cost or below) at year end.

WHAT DO YOU DO WITH YOUR OLD CAR?

This is definitely something you must determine before you go shopping for a lease. Theoretically, it's better to sell your car yourself. You almost always make more money. Most people are aware of this. And, after discovering what a dealer will pay them in trade, many of them try to sell the car through the newspaper—only to have such a miserable time of it that they come back later and trade it in.

When selling your own car, you need some luck, or you may spend many hours waiting for people who never show up. And you need to know how to price the car, or you may spend weeks waiting for phone calls that never come.

Determining the Value of Your Old Car

First, I suggest you forget about consumer used car price guides. Then forget whatever your banker, your insurance agent, or your brother-in-law may have told you. Then forget about the books your banker or insurance agent may have shown you.

Now, find out which used car price guides are used by the car stores and wholesalers in your area—especially the ones used by wholesalers. Wholesalers buy used cars both at auction and from new car dealers, then resell them to used car dealers. They live or die by the prices they put on cars.

The price guides we used were the NADA—or *National Automobile Dealers Association—Official Used Car Guide*, nicknamed the Yellow Book (sometimes available in libraries or from the Guild Department of NADA, 8400 West Park Drive, MacLean, VA 22102 (703) 821-7000). We also used *The Black Book*, the real name and a trademark of the Hearst Business Media Corporation, which publishes it. (National Auto Research Division, P.O. Box 758, Gainesville, GA 30503. Subscription only. (404) 532-4111). Another wholesale price guide is *The Automotive Market Report*.

There is only one version of *The Black Book* and it's the real deal. NADA, however, puts out a consumer version of the Yellow Book. In general, be careful with consumer used car guides, even with the NADA consumer book. When we were unsure of a car's cash value after looking at the professional NADA book's prices, we'd double-check with *The Black Book*.

The Black Book, which comes out every week, was used where I worked and by the local wholesalers; in that area, it was the most accurate guide to the cash value of used cars. But it's no good if it's not used where you live. Find its equivalent at a car store or a lease store and get someone to let you look at it.

Read the directions and observe the classifications. Take some care with this. There may be low mileage allowances, and high mileage deductions. There will be big—that is, great big—deductions for diesel engines. There may be additions for certain options. There will be deductions for the lack of certain options. Make sure you deduct for options your car doesn't have.

Then find the value of your car in one of four typical classifications: rough, average, clean, or extra-clean. Try to be accurate about the car's condition. Bear in mind that average is, after all, what most cars actually are.

After the Book, the Real World

Once you have determined the book value of your car, you should go out into the world and see what reality says. But why bother with the book if you have to go out and face reality anyway? To help keep reality from pulling real wool over your eyes, that's why. In this case, used car dealers constitute reality.

Ugh. This may seem like an incredible chore to you, but it's easy. All you have to do is drive around to three or four used car dealers. A couple little ones and a couple big ones.

If you want to make things easier with a little white lie, tell them you work for a new car dealer and are shopping the car for a customer who wants to trade it in. Then say, "Whatta ya gimme for it?" Or whatever a person like you would say.

They may say they don't want the car or they may quote a price. If you get a price, say, "How do you figure that?" Then, however they justify their price, complain and ask for another two hundred.

See what they say. They might go the deuce, they might go a hun, they might say no and tell you why, they might just shrug and walk away.

Whatever they do, you've got your first offer on the car. Your first price. After you get two or three more and compare them with the book, you will know the wholesale value of your car, its worth in hard dollars, its actual cash value. In short, the price no one will exceed if you trade it in.

But what if you want to sell the car yourself?

To establish your markup, drive around to new car dealers and find out what they are asking for used cars like yours. Go to large new car dealers. Don't visit Smilin' Sam's Used Cars, or Dealin' Dan's Pre-owned Beauties. You can get wholesale from these guys, but not retail. The new car dealer's used car prices will be more predictable and more easily understood. For, generally speaking, his prices will have a closer relation to the quality of the cars. Normally, large new car dealers will fix up a used car and put a warranty on it (to cover most of the cost of surprise repairs) before the car goes over the curb. A new car dealer will do this because he has more to lose by selling junk than many of the Dealin' Dans of the world.

Be sure to see more than one or two cars. And take care not to let your hopes run away with your head when you see the prices on the dealers' cars. Remember, the dealers' easy price for the cars will be $300 to $400 lower than the numbers you see. And he will take off quite a few hundred more for a tough customer. Also remember the things the dealer will do but you won't: detailing, repairs, inspection and warranty. If you don't do those things, you probably won't get the money for them, which amounts to a minimum of $150 to $200.

Even though there's an ass for every seat, only a true boob will pay you as much as he will pay a dealer for the same car. So if your buyer starts haggling, and you have to drop your price, keep in mind this $400 to $500 difference in value between your car and the dealer's. But you can indeed put it on before you take it off. The trick is to overprice so you can discount, but not to price yourself out of the market. Advertise at about $150 less than the average dealer price you've found, and you should get phone calls.

If you do sell your own car, try to get your head straight about price. Some people feel, "My car's worth x thousand dollars. If I don't get it, I ain't selling."

These are the people who come back to the dealership and trade in. Their cars are now worth a few hundred less than they were the first time they came to the dealership. So shoot for the moon, but if you want to move the unit, settle for something reasonable. You do not want to be stuck with the car for months, paying dollar after dollar to keep it registered and insured—which in some areas can run $30 to $40 a week—as you watch dollar after dollar fall off its value.

Questions to Ask Yourself

Are you comfortable with selling things? Many people are not. While others, without even being aware of it, are so blindly enthusiastic that they are terrific natural salespeople.

Do you need a car to drive if the old one sells before you get a new one? Do you have enough space to store the car? Enough time to sell it? If you don't have much time or space, you had better price low and be ready to drop.

If you don't feel comfortable with selling, or you need a new car the moment you let go of the old one, or you have very little time or space, you'll have to forgo the extra money you can make from selling it yourself (but also the potential migraine) and trade it in. For the finer art of this deal, see "A Deal with a Trade" on page 189.

WHERE TO LEASE

Picking the place to lease a car isn't all that easy. Not only is a lease deal more complicated than a buy, but, since lease stores are definitely worth checking out, there are simply more places to call or visit. However, I would suggest starting with dealerships.

Dealerships

Unlike lease stores, dealers are married to manufacturers. Visit a dealership and you'll get your first price from a place that, theoretically, stands behind and services its product, and whose policy, or official policy, is to keep you happy in order to earn your repeat business and to retain the manufacturer's franchise.

Begin with a big dealer, as close to home as possible, that has reputation for dealing: one that advertises itself as a high-volume, low-profit store. (If, however, you live in an area where the stores are few and far between and the dealers act like they're giving away their cabin cruisers when they knock a hundred dollars off a price, call a lease store first. Get the lease store's price and payment quote before visiting the dealership.)

Why start with the big guy, who has to pay all that overhead?

First, at a big dealership, you'll be able to see and handle more cars. This may make it easier to decide on color, options, and so on.

Second, you need some kind of starting price to serve as a benchmark or basis for comparison. With most big dealers, as with most retail stores, size means volume and volume means discounts. Or, at least, the possibility of discounts.

Third, and probably most important, size indicates a desire to grow.

To grow, a store has to get more cars from the manufacturer. And it cannot get them simply by asking. To get more cars, the store has to sell its allotment or more than its allotment. It has to sell everything it is currently getting before the factory will ship it more. A dealer who wants to grow will usually sell for a small profit simply to move the unit — so he can get more units to move.

Obviously, the store you visit should have a reputation for honesty and good service. Check with the Better Business Bureau. Ask friends, relatives, acquaintances, people you work with.

Next, this big, high-volume dealer that enjoys a good reputation and is located near your house should sell the manufacturer's lease program. I think it's a good idea to use the price and payment derived from the manufacturer's lease program for your benchmark, your first point of comparison.

The factory credit companies are big, rich institutions: they are actually more stable than many banks and their pricing and policies will be relatively stable. With Ford Credit, Chrysler Credit, GMAC, Nissan Credit, or Toyota Credit you know, more or less, what you are dealing with: subsidiaries of the manufacturers.

Thus, they have to be a little sensitive to your feelings about your deal. If you have bad feelings about the deal, you may well have bad feelings about your car, a car built by their employer. Banks and lease stores may not care if you become alienated from the factory's products because you were fooled by a lease contract. But Ford and General Motors care; therefore, so do Ford Credit and GMAC.

They're not going to feed your cat and water your plants for you, of course. But take that guy I hammered on the truck lease. Five hundred over sticker. Sold, signed, and delivered. A month after he took the truck, Ford Credit mailed him a new contract. It charged him a lower payment, essentially leasing him the truck at sticker price. A bank wouldn't have bothered.

What to Look for at a Dealership

Look for the signs that indicate good management, such as cleanliness and orderliness; cheerful and friendly personnel; up-to-date, well-maintained facility and equipment; and so on.

Check the hours that the service department is open. Longer hours means more convenience for you. And longer hours also means more mechanics and thus a better chance for prompt service.

After you lease your car, the most important thing about the dealership will be how fast and how well the service department can fix it if it breaks.

Warning Signs: Dealer Add-ons

Dealer addenda, or dealer add-ons, are things the dealer adds to the car whether you want them or not, then charges you for.

Probably the most common of the add-ons is a "protection package" composed of rust proofing, paint shield, fabric guard, and, sometimes, sound deadening. The next most common is striping. Sometimes there's a lot of big, wide striping and some other stuff, which all add up to a "decor group." Retail prices on protection packages and decor groups represent a markup of 200 to 300 percent.

Suppose you want no part of a protection package. But the car you want at the dealer most convenient for you has a sticker on the window saying the stuff is already installed.

Look in the wheel wells and under the hood to see if the metal parts wear a thin coating of yellowish goop. This would be the rustproofing, and there's a chance it won't be there. The window sticker may be a bluff, designed to fake you into thinking you have to pay for all this stuff and give the dealer an extra $400 or so profit on the car.

Why might it be a bluff? Because in a competitive market, no dealer likes to spend even one nickel on a car before someone has committed to buying it.

But if the rustproofing has been sprayed on the car and if the salesperson tells you that you can't get one of their cars without the protection package, leave. That protection package (which should be called a "profit package") will cost the dealer $175 to $200, mostly for the insurance policies behind the warranties. The price to you, however, will probably be $600 to $700.

Don't mess around, don't dicker, don't listen to the salesperson if she tells you she will take the price of the package off the price of the car. She's giving you a phony discount of $600 or so (real discount of around $200) to club you with when you ask for big dollars off the price of the car.

Walk out and go somewhere else.

Leasing Companies or Lease Stores

After you've found a dealership or two with reasonably good reputations for honesty and quality of service, you have another alternative to consider.

Lease stores take your description of car and options, then come up with a price and a payment. If you accept the deal and order the car, the lease store gets it from a car store, delivers it to you, collects your front money, and presents you with a lease contract to sign. Afterward, like dealerships, most will assign the lease to a bank, which pays the lease store, sends you a coupon book, and collects your payments. A few leasing companies finance the deals themselves, sometimes by borrowing from a bank then making payments to the bank out of the payments you make to them.

Lease Stores' Advertising Claims

Note: A growing number of lease stores are on the Internet and, for the most part, they operate just like lease stores that are not on-line. If a leasing company advertises on the Internet, give it a call and get a payment quote. Then check it carefully. On-line advertising is precisely that: advertising. It does not guarantee lower prices or better service.

The advantages lease stores claim in their ads, whether in print or on-line, are these:

1. Wider selection.
2. No high-pressure sales tactics.
3. Lower price.

An advantage they don't advertise is this. Unlike dealerships, many lease stores will quote prices over the phone. The reputable ones give you accurate quotes, for lease stores sell prices not cars. This makes it easier to compare one against another, and also to construct for yourself a range, an array of prices and payments, which makes it easier to compare everybody against everybody else.

Let me poke a few holes in the advertised advantages so you know what to be skeptical about.

Ad claim: wider selection — Lease stores are not franchisees of any particular manufacturer. They will lease you any brand of car that they can obtain from a dealership. But so will many dealerships. The East Babbitt Ford store would lease you a Cadillac or a Mercedes if you wanted one. But we didn't advertise the fact. The problem with the wider selection at the lease store is that you can't see or handle the merchandise at the same place you do the deal. You have to go to two places.

Ad claim: no high-pressure sales tactics — Most lease stores employ salespeople who work on commission. If you don't encounter some form of pressure, you have stumbled across a salesperson who has lost the will to live.

Ad claim: lower price — Maybe, maybe not. When you call lease stores, some will tell you that they can beat a dealer's price because they buy cheap due to the manufacturer's fleet incentive program. The salesperson will say he can lease you a car for a lower price than any dealer will offer.

He may be right. But that doesn't make the rest of what he says necessarily and completely true. First, as mentioned, fleet incentives vary. Try to find out how much the discount actually is. Then, if it's more than $100 or so, find out, or figure out, how much of it is being taken off the price to you.

Second, payments vary, too. Check the leasing company's payment carefully. The bank financing the deal may charge more or less than the factory credit company; or more or less than the bank financing a local car store's leases. Even if the lease store's price sounds unbeatable, you must comparison shop the payment.

So, as with a dealership, find out how many lenders the place uses and who they are. If more than one, compare payments from each. Remember, I had to ask three times to find out about this. And it's worth the effort, for payments can vary as much as $20 a month from bank to bank.

Like a dealer, a leasing company will prefer the lender that pays it the most, not the one that is best for you. And, as we shall see, even stores owned by reputable institutions may employ complicated tricks to hide the true markup. Like car stores, lease stores don't "give" you a good deal. You have to get one.

Finally, since many lease stores are simply offices, check, and check carefully, to determine who will perform warranty repairs on your car. I stress this because dealers often feel that manufacturers pay too little for warranty work, and therefore prefer not to do it. That preference could lead to this scenario:

You get a great payment from a small leasing company. The salesperson says — and you confirm — that an agreement exists with a dealership to provide repair work under the warranty. The little lease store goes out of business. Your car breaks. You call the service department at the dealership.

The service writer tells you they are no longer doing warranty work for the little, defunct lease store's customers. Now what?

Other Disadvantages with Lease Stores

- Many lease stores have no service departments.
- Some do not accept trade-ins.
- At some stores, the people may not know anything about cars. At other lease stores, however, there will be people who know a whole lot about cars.
- If the store doesn't hold its own paper, it has no need for you when the deal is done.
- Lease stores are not disciplined by a manufacturer.
- Some lease stores are started on a fast shuffle and a muttered prayer. Your store may go out of business a few months after you do your deal.

All of this can add up to a lot of inconvenience. And a great big headache if you need repair work done under the manufacturer's warranty. Then you'll have to go to a dealer who may treat you as if you were a three-headed bug.

Some dealerships will do warranty work on cars bought elsewhere; others try very hard to avoid it. And if the schedule is crowded, any dealer will assign your problems a lower priority than a customer's. You may not like this, but if you were in the dealer's shoes, you would do the same thing.

So when considering a lease store:

- See if it can handle your trade-in, if you have one.
- Find out how long it has been in business — and try to

make an estimate of the probability it will stay in business. You may not be an investment banker, but go with your gut feeling.

· Ask if the store has a service arrangement with a repair shop or a dealership. If the answer is yes, call the shop or dealership. Make sure the arrangement exists, make sure it will last the entire length of your warranty and/or lease term, and make sure you are not paying extra for it.

Do the Advantages Outweigh the Disadvantages?
If you want a car not handled by any of the local car stores, yes, obviously, you have no choice.

If you are in an area where the car stores are few and far between—and therefore try to eliminate discounts—quite possibly. A smart lease store working with a smart bank may offer payments that blow the local dealers out of the water.

Character may give you an answer. A half mile away from your house, the most honest and helpful guy in town may be running a lease store that's been in business for twenty years.

If the place you're considering checks out, all that's left to consider is the economics of the deal.

THE ECONOMICS OF THE DEAL

Here's a checklist to help you compare.

Closed- or open-end lease

Amount of security deposit

MSRP

Factory discounts

Sticker price

Store discount

Sell price

Lease or interest rate

Residual value factor (percentage of MSRP)

Residual value amount

Payment

Lease-end purchase option?

Any charge for purchase option?

Lease-end buyout amount

Total cost if you don't buy at lease end

Total cost if you do buy at lease end

Option to buy during term?

Prepayment penalties? How much?

What happens in case of total loss?

Gap insurance available? How much?

Condition of car at end of term: any zingers?

Liability and collision insurance requirement

Number of miles included in payment

Excess mileage penalty (if applicable)

Trade allowance (if applicable)

Cash value offered for your trade (if applicable)

Disposition fee? How much?

With this information, you should be able to make a pretty full comparison between different cars and different deals.

Note: If you want the performance model of a standard nameplate, you may have to look harder for a good deal. Assuming performance cars will be abused, many lenders lower their residuals 3% to 5% below the standard models. This raises the lease payment significantly.

In the used car market, however, these relatively rare vehicles are more much expensive than standard models with comparable amenities. Even at wholesale, they bring thousands more. Some lenders take this into account, but you may have to search to find them. As before, if low payment is your primary concern, shop for the highest residual. If convinced you'll buy the vehicle and have some flexibility on the payment, shop for the deal with the least overall cost.

The Relationship Between Price and Payment

Whatever kind of car you want, be sure to double-check the relationship between the sell price and the payment. As we shall see, one place may charge you a higher sell price than another, charge you a higher lease rate, use the same residual value, and yet charge you the same, or even less, per month—which adds up to charging you the same, or less, period.

This can happen because different lenders use different methods of calculating, or, more accurately, inflating lease payments.

Since payments can be inflated, the relationship between price and payment is not necessarily constant.

Therefore, do not follow the advice on leasing sometimes given by apparently knowledgeable people: to concentrate only on the vehicle's price. Simply put, that's wrong. It can cost you.

You do need to pay attention to price. You do need to force the salesperson to quote price accurately. Then you need to do what the salesperson or manager does: move fluidly between cost, price, cash difference (if there's a trade), and payment.

If you lose sight of any of the elements in the deal, you are likely to be fooled. Not because anyone is going to do anything special in your case, but just as a matter of routine. As we shall see in our tale of Josie (in chapter 6), some salespeople quote payments so far beyond what you need to pay that it's almost obscene. They wouldn't do this if it didn't work.

How to Calculate Lease Payments

To avoid being fooled and thus to save money when you lease a car, you must be able to calculate payments. Trying to find out what's going on by acting suspicious, playing the role of the "tough customer," and trying to force your salesperson and/or manager to explain everything will not necessarily result in either the truth or a good deal.

Consider again my truck lease customer, Paul, from the introduction. After showing him lease charts and buy charts and the factor for this and the factor for that, we showed him the factor for 9.5% (the rate he was being charged) and told him how to figure out the principal on a loan. Then we divided the factor into his lease payment and came up with a principal two thousand dollars less than the price of the truck. That, we told him, was what he was paying for the truck. Two thousand dollars off! Was that a super discount, or what?

His suspicion evaporated. He had to admit it. It was one hell of a discount. It was damn near the deal of the century. He took the deal, took the truck, and went away happy. And, as I said, this guy was not dumb. Far from it, in fact. He just didn't know the numbers.

Here, then, are the numbers: some of the methods of calculating lease payments. One is the way we did it on the deals we put through Ford Credit. Another is the no-frills "basic method," also called the "depreciation method." Since most lenders add frills to squeeze extra juice from the basic method, the third is from the gigantic bank that financed our 60-month leases. This "bank method" is like the basic one, but makes it obvious where the extra juice comes from: the addition of a $200 bank fee. In appendix B, you will find sample charts containing examples of residual value factors.

Although there are other methods of calculation, these are highly typical. If you figure a payment on a Kia, a Chevy, or a Porsche using these methods, you should be very close. If you are not very close, you should take the trouble to find out why. Two things you should understand going in:

1. Most lease payments—even when you get a good deal—have a little extra juice, or profit, built in. For example, using a financial calculator to figure out the payment on our sample Escort ($11,800 sell price, $4,662 residual, 8.5% lease rate, 48-month term) will yield a monthly payment of $207.49.

Ford calls the extra money contained in payments derived with its factors an "administrative fee." The fee is calculated by adding 1/10th of one percent of the capitalized cost to the payment (but not charging interest on it.)

Other lenders may use different terminology and calculations. Some hide those calculations, some simply add a bank fee. What's the bank fee for? Nothing. Nothing that is, but extra profit for the bank. It is in essence prepaid interest added to the deal in such a way that the bank does not have to call it interest. We can, however, keep the concept and the terms consistent from lender to lender by looking at the juice as if it comes from either a higher sell price or a lower residual value.

Thus, if you raise the Escort's sell price by $481.50, the calculator will show a before tax payment of $219.28, within a penny of our friend, $219.29, from chapter Two.

Or, if you retain the $11,800 sell price and use a residual of $3,985 the calculator will give $219.30, again within a penny of $219.29. Incidentally, you might be interested to know that $3,985 is a much easier price to get for that Escort when it comes off the lease than $4,662. We'll talk more about this later.

2. Lease rates and residual values change. Lease rates may go down, up, and down again by the time you read this. What you have here are tools with which to learn and compare, not gospel. In this kind of simple math, the gospel is in the formulae and relationships, not the numbers. If you learn how to calculate lease payments on a $10,000 car, you could use the method on a $50,000 car and be right on the money.

How We Did It at the East Babbit Ford Store

Here's how we figured payments on the leases we wrote through Ford Motor Credit:

Residual Value and Residual Value Factor— The residual value factor is the percentage of MSRP used to calculate the dollar amount of a car's residual or lease-end value after the amount of time the lease will run. To find it, call a Ford dealer, a dealership selling the brand you want, a lease store, or a bank. They'll tell you: residuals are not kept secret.

Multiply MSRP before package discounts by the factor, which, for the Monte Carlo, would be 34%. We'll multiply the Monte's MSRP of $18,345 by that, then, calculate a payment a la Ford Credit. We'll find that it's a good bit higher than the payment from the bank we used previously.

Because .34 times $18,345 equals $6,237, we find, then, that the Monte Carlo's residual value after four years is $6,237.

Residual Value Credit Factor— Now we would consult a chart from Ford Credit. What you would do is call or visit a Ford dealer and play "footsy" with a salesperson or the leasing manager. They will have a chart with two columns of factors. One will contain the acquisition cost (or capitalized cost) payment factors. The other, our concern for the moment, will hold the residual value or lease-end value credit (or deduction) factors.

Footsy is an implied promise of future business. If you are at a Ford dealership, talk the salesperson into telling you what the factors are for the current interest rate and length of lease term you want. (Get factors for longer and shorter terms and higher and lower rates, too. And if the salesperson is helpful, what the heck, you may as well deliver on your implied promise.) Write down the factors.

Now, the residual value credit factor is used to determine how much will be deducted from the acquisition cost payment to compensate for the car's value at the end of the lease.

To get that amount, multiply the residual value by the residual, or lease-end, value credit factor. For a 48-month lease with a rate of 8.5%, Ford's factor is .017441. On the Monte Carlo, then, the residual value of $6,237 is multiplied by .017441, which equals $108.77. This residual value credit will be subtracted from the acquisition cost payment to arrive at the lease payment.

Acquisition Cost, Acquisition Cost Payment Factor, and Acquisition Cost Payment— Some lenders use the term "capitalized cost" or "cap cost" to mean the same thing as "acquisition cost." Both terms refer to the capital the lender/lessor puts out to acquire the car and that you partially pay off (plus interest, of course) to acquire the lease on the car. Acquisition cost or capitalized cost is calculated as follows:

MSRP _____
minus Package discounts (if any) − _____
equals Sticker price = _____
minus Store discount − _____
equals Sell price = _____
minus Cash down (if any, from you or from a factory rebate) and/or trade equity put down (if any) − _____
plus Balance owed on trade (if any) + _____
plus Cost of dealer add-ons or any extras you purchase + _____
equals Capitalized (or acquisition) cost = _____

The Monte Carlo began with an MSRP of $18,345. A factory rebate and our teriffic negotiating skills took us down to a sell price of $16,500. We put nothing down, we traded nothing in, we owed nothing, we bought nothing extra, so the sell price of $16,500 was our acquisition cost.

To get the acquisition cost factor, we have asked at the dealership (or looked it up, if we have the charts). For 48 months at a lease rate of 8.5%, Ford's factor is .025475. Multiply the acquisition or capitalized cost by this factor to derive the acquisition cost payment.

That is, $16,500 × .025475 = $420.34, our acquisition cost payment.

Monthly Lease Payment— To get the monthly payment, we subtract the residual value credit from the acquisition cost payment.

So $420.34 − $108.77 = $311.57, the Ford Motor Credit before-tax lease payment based on our $16,500 price.

Summary

1. The MSRP, before factory discounts, multiplied by the residual value factor equals the residual value.
2. The discounted price minus any cash or trade equity put down (plus balance owed on the trade, if any) equals the acquisition or capitalized cost.
3. Acquisition or capitalized cost multiplied by the acquisition cost payment factor from the chart or salesperson equals the acquisition cost payment.
4. The residual value amount multiplied by the residual value "credit" factor equals the residual value deduction from the acquisition payment.
5. Acquisition payment minus this deduction equals the lease payment.

The Basic Method (or Depreciation Method)

Most lenders look for a little extra money in different parts of the deal, but here's the method most of them start with. The lease payment is divided into two parts.

1. You pay off the estimated amount that the car will depreciate during the lease (or amortize the depreciation).

2. You pay interest, also known as lease charges. That interest, computed using the money factor, or lease factor, is charged on the "total money" (capitalized cost plus residual value) that the lender considers to be at risk.

The capitalized cost is derived as just shown. And so is the residual value. But each lender decides for itself what percentage will be used as the residual value factor and each lender has its own charts printed up. You have to call around to find out what factors your lenders are using, just as you must call to find out what their lease rates are.

Summary of the Depreciation Method

1. Capitalized cost minus residual value amount equals depreciation.
2. Depreciation divided by the number of months in the lease equals the monthly depreciation payment.
3. Capitalized cost plus residual value equals total money.
4. Total money multiplied by the money or lease factor equals the monthly interest payment or monthly lease charge.
5. Monthly depreciation plus monthly interest payment equals your monthly lease payment. Plus tax.

Here's how to calculate the payment on the Monte Carlo lease, using Ford's residual value and interest rate:

Sell price equals capitalized cost—no down payment and no balance to be paid off)	$16,500.00
Residual value	−$6,237.00
48 months' depreciation	=$10,263.00

Monthly depreciation payment	$213.81
($10,263.00 ÷ 48)	

Capitalized cost	$16,500.00
Residual value	+$6,237.00
Total money	=$22,737.00
Money factor (.00354 for 8.5% lease rate)	×.00354
Monthly interest payments	=$80.49

Monthly depreciation payment	$215.26
Monthly interest payment	+$80.24
Monthly lease payment	=$295.50

The payment is seventeen dollars a month lower than Ford's. We saw that Ford factors have a built-in administrative charge. You cannot, however, say to your Ford salesman, "You're wrong," because Ford can figure out its factors however it wants. What you can say, after you figure out what the residual value would be, based on that payment, is, "I want my guaranteed buyout to be the same as the residual used to calculate the payment." Or, "I think I can beat that payment. Is it the best you can do?"

The Bank Method

Like Ford, and like most banks, the one that financed our 60-month deals added a bank fee to the capitalized cost, effectively raising the sell price of the car. The one we used charged $200. Some banks charge more, some less; some charge no fee, and some charge no stated fee but have hidden charges built into their calculations.

This bank charged a lease rate 1% higher than Ford. So the lease rate here of 9.5% and its money factor of .00396 appear high. Notice in the following example, however, that while the rate is not competitive, the payment is—because the residual value is high and because the stated residual is actually used to calculate the payment.

Here's how the Monte Carlo calculations would have looked if put through that particular bank, which, incidentally, called the capitalized cost plus bank fee the "net agreed value":

Sell price	$16,500.00
Bank fee	+$200.00
Net agreed value (capitalized or acquisition cost)	=$16,700.00
Residual value (40% of $18,435 MSRP)	−$7,338.00
48 months' depreciation	=$9,362.00
Monthly depreciation payment ($9,444 ÷ 48)	$194.05
Net agreed value	$16,700.00
Residual value	+$7,338.00
Total money	=$24,038.00
Money factor (.00396 for 9.5% lease rate)	×.00396
Monthly interest payment	=$95.19
Monthly depreciation payment	$195.04
Monthly interest payment	+$95.19
Monthly lease payment	=$290.23

As you can see, the payment is *highly* competitive. Why? At the time we were dealing with them, this bank was eager for lease business. Therefore, they used residual values that were not merely high, they were from LaLa Land.

And that's what to look for when shopping for a good lease deal: a residual value from LaLa Land.

If you find one, however, be careful to check that:

1. It is actually used to calculate the payment.
2. It's a percentage of MSRP, not the sell price—i.e., that both the residual factor (the percentage) *and* the dollar amount are high. For a formula could be worked out using a high percentage of a low dollar amount, resulting in a low residual and a high lease payment.

Also check that the contract does not require you to return a car in clean retail condition. You want it to require average condition. Average is not clean. The difference starts at about $500 and rises swiftly. And if the lease requires a clean car and yours is average, that difference comes from you.

How to Derive the Money Factor

In our examples we've seen money factors of .00354 and .00396. The money factor equals one half the nominal monthly interest rate. You derive it by dividing the quoted interest rate or lease rate by 12 and then by 2—or simply by 24.

Thus 9.5% (or .095) divided by 24 equals .0039583. Rounded up in the lender's favor this equals .00396 (or, quite possibly, .004). And 8.5% (.085) divided by 24 = .00354. If you know the money factor and want the nominal lease or interest rate, you perform the reverse operation.

So .00396 × 24 = .09504, or 9.5%, give or take.

And .00354 × 24 = .08496, or 8.5%.

Or you can skip the decimal places and divide or multiply by 2,400.

Work through the very simple arithmetic laid out above. Practice with different prices and residuals.

Do it! Learning is like love. The first jolt comes easy, but afterwards, if you won't work for it, it won't work for you.

And don't worry if it isn't second nature to you. Although the arithmetic is easy, the concepts, and the sequence of concepts, may be new and may take a little getting used to.

Then, before going out to shop price, calculate lease payments on a whole range of prices, from 10 percent over sticker all the way down to cost and below. We'll talk more about this in the chapter on doing the deal.

Suppose, when you are actually doing the deal, the payments quoted to you seem somehow "off"?

Have the salesperson go through the calculations with you. Check and verify each factor and each step.

If the salesperson doesn't know how to calculate lease payments (a surprisingly large number don't) a manager will be doing it for him/her. In that case, have him/her get the manager to demonstrate the calculations to you. A slip of the finger on a calculator button could cost you a nice piece of change.

If your salesperson is unwilling to do this, then he/she's not willing to work hard enough to earn you business. Tell them so, in exactly those words. They have been taught, repeatedly, that it takes hard work to earn a customer's business, so saying that should push a button.

And now that we know a little about what we're doing, let's talk briefly about advertisements, then put our knowledge into action and do some shopping.

READING THE ADS

Many people start to shop by sitting down. Then they read the ads in the newspaper.

PAINLESS PAYMENTS!   LEASE IT OR LOSE IT!
LUXURY FOR LESS!   SAVE! SAVE! SAVE!!!

What do car ads tell you? Not much. The most useful information appearing in car ads in the newspapers is news about factory cash rebates and factory subsidized low interest rates. But there are a few pieces of information the ads may communicate.

1. You can get an idea of the relative prices of cars.

For example, the Sunday automotive section advertised a Pontiac Bonneville 4-door for $23,793. A bit further on, is a Mercury Grand Marquis for $21,995. The Marquis has an "older" image. Am I that old? If I am, the Marquis should give my old bones a cushier, more couch-like ride and save me some buckaroos.

On the other hand, if I'm young at heart and want a four-by-four so I can gaze commandingly over the tops of other cars in the mall parking lot, here's an Isuzu Trooper at $329 a month, nothing down, for a three-year, 12,000 mile per year lease.

But on another page is a Nissan Pathfinder for $299, also nothing down, three years, at 15,000 miles a year. Is the Trooper worth an extra $30 a month and fewer allowable miles?

2. You can get an idea of which dealers are dealing low.

A few pages further on, I see a Nissan Altima advertised, no money down, 36-month lease, for $241, before taxes. On the next page is the same model, same lease terms, at $237. Whoops, here's another one: same car, same deal, $234 a month. If I were in the market for an Altima, I'd stop first at the dealer who advertised $234.

Conversely, here's an ad for a Chevy Lumina. MSRP is listed as $16,159. Sale price is $15,330 with an asterisk. The asterisked small print says sale price includes $500 first-time buyer rebate where applicable. So the actual sale price is $15,830; $329 below sticker. A dealer who thinks a $329 discount is a hot deal is out of his mind. And so this dealer would get pushed to the end of the list of stores to visit if I were looking for a Lumina.

3. You may be able to get an idea of the relative cost of lease payments for different vehicles.

For example, the Altimas mentioned above had standard transmissions. But now I notice an automatic Pontiac Grand Am for only $212 a month. So, maybe I'll get the Grand Am. . . .

Then I look at the small print, which in this particular ad is very small indeed. It tells me that the Grand Am lease is for 12,000 miles a year (the Altimas are 15,000) and requires $2,000 down. Whoa! Over 36 months that's $55.55 per month plus $5 or $6 interest, so the cost of a no-money-down lease would be about $272 per month. Since I can get the Altima with an automatic for $249 a month, no money down, the question becomes, is the Grand Am worth $23 a month more?

Do be careful to compare the lease terms in the small print.

The Rest of the Stuff in the Ads: Common Come-ons
The basic technique of car ads is the bait and switch. Something wonderful provokes your excitement and desire — but turns out to be unavailable. Your excitement is then refocused, and your desire switched to something else. Here are a few of its more common forms.

Price and Payment for One Car Only— You see a terrific lease payment in great big print. But when you read the tiny print you find a stock number or VIN (Vehicle Identification Number—i.e., serial number). When the store identifies the advertised vehicle with a number, that particular vehicle is the only one the store is legally obligated to sell at the advertised price. That vehicle may be the most unpopular color of the decade. Or it may be exactly what you want. If it is, there's a good chance that it will have already been sold.

Price and Payment Excluding Freight Charges— This little number was the favorite of the store that was five minutes down the road from ours—the store that came in either right behind us or right ahead of us in Ford's monthly sales figures. Of course, the ad does tell you that freight is excluded from the ad price. In the tiny print.

Payment Calculated with Cash Down— This was our favorite. (And it has grown extremely common.) We advertised fabulous payments in big, bold graphics. Down at the bottom, the small print would say that the payment was based on a down payment of thousands of dollars in cash or trade equity.

Excited customers would walk in waving the newspaper and ask eagerly to see the car. The moment always came, however, when the salesman would have to acquaint the customer with the facts. Then you'd hear the customer start to yell. Then you'd see the customer walk out.

Lease Payment Based on a Low Mileage Allowance— This one is growing in popularity as the prices of cars continue their extraordinary climb. You see a payment figure that gets you all excited. Then in the extremely tiny print you find that the payment is based on an allowance of 9,000—or even 7,500—miles a year.

The Mystery Vehicle with the Magic Residual — This gimmick promotes a bank lease program or a factory lease program, rather than a particular car. The ad will mention an unnamed vehicle at some price and with some residual value. If you take the trouble to discover what percentage of price the residual represents, you will find the percentage to be extremely high. So high, in fact, that perhaps only three percent of the cars in existence retain their value that well. You thus have three chances in a hundred that the car you want will have a payment similar to the one in the ad.

Ad gimmicks are more common than houseflies. Don't be fooled. Do not count on advertised sale prices to save you money. Look for the kick in the head in the tiny print. If it isn't there, be prepared for it when you go to the store. Remember, as long as supply exceeds demand, you can lease a car yesterday or tomorrow for the price that is advertised as today's only. If you know how.

A FORM TO HELP CALCULATE LEASE PAYMENTS

MSRP   _____
times Residual value factor   × _____
equals RESIDUAL VALUE   = _____

Selling price   _____
plus Bank fee (if any)   + _____
equals Adjusted selling price   = _____
plus Extras purchased   + _____
minus Cash or trade put down   − _____
equals CAPITALIZED COST   = _____

Capitalized cost   _____
minus Residual value   − _____
equals DEPRECIATION   = _____

Depreciation amount   _____
divided by Months in lease   ÷ _____
equals MONTHLY DEPRECIATION
    PAYMENT   = _____

Capitalized cost   _____
plus Residual value   + _____
equals TOTAL MONEY   = _____

Total money   _____
times Money factor
   (interest rate divided by 2,400)   × _____
equals MONTHLY INTEREST PAYMENT   = _____

Monthly depreciation payment   _____
plus Monthly interest payment   + _____

equals MONTHLY LEASE PAYMENT   = _____

Plus tax, of course: either the tax rate times the monthly payment, or the tax rate times the total of the monthly payments, if your state collects the tax up front.

Do Your Homework and Then Take Your Time

It may sound as if you are in for a nightmare when you go out to lease a car. Not so. I've done many deals that were pleasant all the way through and resulted in good bargains and happy customers. In these instances, however, the customers almost always knew what they were doing and made sure they had plenty of time to do it. This is important. Hurrying costs money.

Once, after a friend had signed a contract on a minivan, I went back to the store with him and saved them $324 in thirty minutes. Another thirty minutes or so would have saved another $300. But my friend was on lunch hour and had to go back to work.

Before giving in to you and accepting your deal, the manager may need to feel that both he and the salesperson have done a good job, that they've done everything they possibly can. This may take a while; both of them may have quite a number of moves to try. But time increases your bargaining power. The more time they spend on you, the more painful it is for them to lose the deal.

What are the chances you'll make a deal on your first visit? Good.

And even better than good if you are knowledgeable and firm. For the manager knows—and has told his salespeople over and over—that if you do walk, there's only one chance in ten that you will ever come back.

Even so, sometimes you have to walk out. Remember the copy machine manager who leased a Taurus station wagon from me at $269 over cost? To do it, he had to walk twice. And a friend of mine had to walk out twice before he got his price on a Mustang GT. Nevertheless, both of them got the deals they wanted. And so will you.

PUTTING IT ALL TOGETHER:
Let's Go Shopping

Everything that you are about to read in this chapter actually happened during the research for the first edition of this book. Only the names of the people and places involved have been changed. I am leaving the incidents—and the numbers—as they were to give you insight into how deals can go, and some of the pitfalls and shams that you may encounter.

So don't be shocked or too concerned about my mental condition when you encounter the 1990 prices below. What you should pay attention to is how those numbers were presented to me and the relationships between the numbers, and how the salespeople presented those numbers to me.

For our research exercise, we are going to lease a Ford Taurus GL for four years. The car has a three-liter V-6 engine, an automatic overdrive transmission, and equipment package 204A, which includes air conditioner, cruise control, tilt steering wheel, power mirrors, power windows, power locks, power driver's seat, rear window defogger, interval wipers, light group, digital clock, a decorative pinstripe, and finned wheel covers.

Options on the car as priced but not included in the package are: whitewall tires, clearcoat paint, and a stereo radio with cassette player. Power steering and brakes are standard. The MSRP is $15,826. A $500 package discount brings the sticker price down to $15,326.

We have bought a cost and price guide and have determined cost on the car as follows:

Base	$10,231
Freight	$426
Optional engine and transmission	$571
Package 204A	$1,537
Whitewalls	$69
Cassette	$116
Clearcoat paint	$155
Subtotal	$13,105
Advertising and finance	$196
Subtotal (invoice cost)	$13,301
Pack	$150
Total (dealer cost)	$13,451

We have also looked over the newspaper ads and discovered that Ford is offering $600 cash back on Tauruses. Mmmm, goody. Since the budget is a little tight, we'll put the rebate down on the car, lowering the acquisition cost by $600. And, finally, we have calculated a range of lease payments, starting at about $1,200 under cost and going up to sticker plus 10 percent. Imagining myself to be us, out I went.

A QUICK PRICE QUOTE

It was a cold, gray day, with scattered snow flurries: your basic slow day at the car store. I parked next to a little pile of snow and went into the showroom. And there was a Taurus with all the right equipment: $15,326.

A young man, around twenty-two, walked up to me and introduced himself. Seemed like a nice guy. He was wearing a white shirt with big, bold stripes and a short-pointed spread collar. His tie was a hair wider than the stripes on the shirt. I said I liked Tauruses and was thinking about buying or leasing one. What would it cost to lease a car like the one sitting right there?

He didn't know, he said, because he was new on the job. But he did know leasing was a great way to go. He said it would save me an awful lot of money.

I knew he was supposed to check with a manager before quoting any numbers. So I asked him if he could find out what it would cost to lease a car like this.

He said that, well, you have to have a specific car in mind. I told him that, except for the color, this one was exactly like the one I wanted. What would it cost to lease it? (You may have to walk the lot to find one like the one you want. If so, do it.)

He dodged the question, asking if I was ready to do a deal today. No, I was just shopping around, trying to find out about leasing and what it would cost. In fact, what would it cost to lease a car exactly like this one here? Could he find out for me?

In dodging my questions, he was merely doing his job. Handing out prices to wandering shoppers is precisely what salespeople are not supposed to do. But since I kept pressing him, he went off to talk to a manager. I stared at the Taurus.

When he came back, he tried another dodge. He said he couldn't find the right person. This was pure bull.

I said, "But I have to have some idea what it would cost to lease. I know all about buying, I've bought [two, five, twelve cars already: pick a number that fits your age] but I have to find out what it would cost me to lease. What would it cost me to lease this car right here?"

Now if the salesperson keeps dancing and dodging, don't make the mistake of getting angry, as more than a few folks do.

Instead, simply persist in being logical. Say that you want to compare leasing and buying. But how can you compare them if you don't know what it would cost to lease the car you want? You can't, that's how. So you need—not "want"—or "have" to know what it would cost to lease the car. In this case, after I repeated that basic message once again, he said:

"Oh, about two-fifty a month."

As you can see, the right person had been there and had given the salesman a number. But he had also given him an order not to mention the number unless he had to.

Now we compare $250 with the figures we've compiled. Cost with pack is $13,451. Adding $400 for profit makes the sell price of $13,851. Subtracting the $600 rebate put down on the car leaves an acquisition cost of $13,251. Using a residual of $5,700, and a 10% lease rate, I calculated the payment several ways and came up with a range of $237 to $245.

So $250 a month is a ballpark figure that's not too bad. There may be too much profit in there ($500 to $600 instead of the $400 I used) but not a lot too much. Now we have a price and we've had a little practice at extracting information from a car salesman who didn't want to give it.

And—a couple of pluses—even though he tried to withhold information, he was a pleasant enough guy; and his price was not an insult. In fact, it was low enough to indicate a willingness to deal. These pluses add up to a car store that deserves careful consideration, and perhaps a return trip. Mission accomplished.

A Lease Store

Unlike dealerships, you can shop lease stores over the phone. So I got out the Yellow Pages and called a few. Two of them financed their own deals.

One of the places was, amazingly, a bank. When the manufacturers' credit arms came aggressively after lease business, many banks folded their tents and went quietly back to mortgages. But in Philadelphia an old, "reputable" bank, which we'll call Third Bank, went whole hog after leasing. The bank not only finances deals for dealers and lease stores, it also runs its own, in-house lease store. We'll call it BankLease.

A bank-owned lease store was new to me, so I paid them a visit. No store, no lot, no garage. Just an office in a midrise bank building plopped down in the middle of a suburban parking lot. They gave me a brochure.

The Brochure

Brochures, as you know, are not textbooks. They are ads. But, despite all my warnings to you about ads, I was sucked in. The brochure gave a comparison between a three-year buy and a three-year lease on a car priced at $18,000. The finance rate on the buy was three-quarters of a percent "above" the current average rate. (This is a trick that enhances the comparison. To spot it, familiarize yourself with current interest rates.) The payment was well beyond what I could afford, over $500 a month. But the 36-month lease payment was $20 a month "less" than everything else I had been looking at.

What a deal! What an incredible deal. I couldn't see how they did it. I felt a rush of desire. I actually thought, Maybe I'll go get this car.

Then, calming down a little, I decided to see if such a good deal were possible. After doing a bunch of calculations using Tauruses, Cutlasses, and Maximas, and using BankLease's residual value chart, which I had lured into my possession, I kept coming up with payments $30 to $40 a month over the one in the brochure. Hmmm. I tried some below-market lease rates and still couldn't get down that low.

Suspicion arose.

Perhaps I was in the presence of a magic payment on a mystery car with a magnificent residual: bait to prime me for the switch.

How did they pull it off? By basing the example on a car that will have a 57% residual value after three years. The charts used would have to be the ones in use at the very beginning of the model year, not the calendar year.

At that time (1990), even on October charts, few to no vehicles carried three-year residuals of 57%. On BankLease's own charts, the highest three-year residuals I could find were: a Honda Prelude at 56%, a couple of Honda Accords at 55%, a Toyota Camry at 55%, BMW's 325ic convertible at 54%, a couple of Acuras at 53%, Ford's Aerostar at 52%, Chevy's Astro Passenger Van at 51%, Dodge's Caravan at 50%. For most cars the 36-month residual, even in October, was between 39% and 47%.

To give you a little more context, on BankLease's October charts, most BMWs (a car supposed to hold its value quite well) had three-year residuals of 45% to 47%: well under the percentage needed to attain the low payment advertised in the brochure. If you went to BankLease for a car, your chances of matching the deal in the ad would be about one in a hundred. But the ad was a triumph. It achieved the ultimate goal of all car ads, in fact, of all advertising. It provoked intense desire. It was completely misleading. It could not be proven false.

Lorna

In the Philadelphia area at that time, the tax on leases was 6%. To see how the bank explained the ad, I called them up. I asked what kind of car the example was based on.

"It's not based on any car," said the woman, whose name was Lorna.

"What do you mean? It has to be based on something."

"Well, it's based on an abstract car. It's, like, an example."

"Oh," I said.

"But if you tell me what kind of car you're looking for, I can work out a real price for you," she said.

So I described the Taurus.

"I'll call you back," said Lorna.

Next day, she did.

She quoted me a four-year lease payment of $261.92, including 6% tax. The deal allowed 15,600 miles per year, or 62,400 miles over the four years. Penalty for excessive mileage was eight cents a mile.

I had my calculator handy, and, simply by dividing 1.06 into the payment, figured out that the before-tax payment for the car was $247.09 per month.

Then I asked what price the payment was based on. And Lorna gave me quite a rundown. Compare the following with what you are told when you ask the same question.

Lorna told me that MSRP was $15,826 and there was a $500 package discount, so retail on the car was $15,326.

Dealer cost, she said, was $13,340. This was about right. I didn't ask if BankLease got a fleet discount—or who was pocketing it if they did. You should ask this, however.

To the $13,340, $75 was added for profit, bringing the deal price or sell price up to $13,415. Then Ford's $600 cash rebate was figured in as a down payment and subtracted, leaving a capitalized cost of $12,815. The residual value was $5,870, which also served, said Lorna, as the guaranteed buyout at the end of the lease.

The quoted price struck me as extremely good. The payment I wasn't sure about yet. I asked about the lease rate, and Lorna told me it was 9.14% (typical lease rates at the time were 9.5% to 10.5%).

"That sounds pretty good," I said.

"It is good," said Lorna. "It's the best deal you can get. No dealer will sell you a car like that for seventy-five over cost."

True enough. "I'll call you back," I said.

Checking the Payment

I talked to Lorna in January and, since I happened to have Ford's January charts, I used them first to check Lorna's payment quote. Ford pegged the Taurus's 48-month residual at 36%, a bit lower than BankLease. Then I called a Ford dealer and found the current Ford lease rate was 9.5%.

As Lorna said she had done, I used the rebate as a down payment, resulting in an acquisition cost of $12,815. I figured residual value at 36% of $15,826, or $5,697.

With these figures and Ford charts, I calculated a payment of $234.98 per month before tax, or $250.38 after tax.

Despite a lower residual value and a lease rate almost

half a percent higher, the Ford Credit payment came to $12 less than BankLease's. Something was funny.

Now, what Lorna said about the price was true. No dealer will sell you a $15,000 car for $75 over cost.

So I added $325, to bring the profit up to $400, which quite a few dealers will accept. Price is now $13,740 and acquisition cost (after subtracting the $600 down) is $13,140. Now the payment came out to $243.41 or $258.01 with tax.

Thus, with a price $325 higher than BankLease's, and with the use of Ford lease charts—which add an administrative fee—the payment was three dollars a month lower than BankLease's.

To check my figures again, I used the price at $400 over cost and calculated a payment using the bank method. The acquisition cost after the rebate is still $13,140, but now I added a $200 bank fee, making it $13,340.

Using BankLease's residual value of $5,870, and a higher money factor of .00425 (lease rate of 10.2%), I came up with a payment of $237.26 a month, or $251.50 with tax.

Again, a higher price and a higher rate than BankLease's, yet a payment of $9.83 less. How could these payments be lower than BankLease's, given BankLease's phenomenal price and rate?

Next, I tried the numbers Lorna quoted, using the basic method. As mentioned, lenders often find this method a bit too basic and add money here and there; your use of it, however, will give you an idea how much has been added.

Sell price	$13,415.00
Cash down	−$600.00
Capitalized cost	$12,815.00

Capitalized cost	$12,815.00
Residual value	−$5,870.00
Depreciation	=$6,945.00

Monthly depreciation payment	$144.69
($6,945 ÷ 48 months)	

Total money ($12,815 + $5,870)	$18,685.00
Money factor	×.0038
Monthly interest payment	=$71.00

Monthly depreciation payment	$144.69
Monthly interest payment	+$71.00
Monthly lease payment	=$215.69

Thirty-one and change under BankLease's payment. What was going on?

Well, they could be lying about the price of the car. Or they could be finagling numbers around so they can misrepresent the price without really lying. Remember, in the Age of the Image, lies are not what they once were. There is only representation, and representation is the play of light on water in fog.

How to Find Out Why the Payment Does Not Match Your Calculations

You should check and verify all of the following—but if it grows too involved, skip to "Lorna Spills the Beans" (page 132) for a vague but wonderful explanation.

First, I had to get additional information.

I called Lorna and told her it seemed like I would be

paying too much money. Then I asked what I was paying off.

"It doesn't work that way," she said.

"How does it work?"

"Leasing gives you a low monthly payment," she said. "If you were buying the car you would be paying—"

"I know, I know," I said, "but what am I paying off?"

Now Lorna grew firm. Stern, even.

"You are not 'paying off,'" she said (a hint of scorn at the very idea), "like you would pay off the principal on a loan. You are paying depreciation plus interest."

"How much depreciation and how much interest?" I said. She told me $171.70 depreciation and $75.39 interest.

171.70 + 75.39 = 247.09, sure enough. That added up okay. But some other things didn't.

Breaking Down the Payment

Let's take a look at the depreciation.

After 48 months (48 × 171.70) total depreciation paid would be $8241.60. For convenience sake, I'll drop the change.

If the acquisition cost is $12,815 and we pay off $8241 in depreciation, then the residual should be $4574, not $5870.

To put it the other way, if the acquisition cost is $12,815 and the residual is $5870, then the deprecation should be $6945. Over a period of 48 months, the monthly depreciation should be $144.69, as we saw in the payment calculation, not $171.70.

I called Lorna again and told her exactly that.

Then I said, "If I pay $8241 depreciation, with a residual of $5870, I'm paying $14,111 for the car. What's going on? I thought I was getting it for $12,815."

(Plus the $600 rebate from Ford, don't forget, which is going down on the car.)

"It doesn't work that way," said Lorna. "You are getting the car for $12,815. Leasing doesn't work on an APR basis."

Lorna showed the dodges of a born saleswoman. Here, she was answering a customer's question with an answer to a different question.

I reminded her that I had just figured it out on a depreciation basis, not an APR basis (as you would figure out a "regular" installment purchase loan).

"Oh," she said, "right. The buyout does seem a little high."

"A little?"

"Well, maybe almost a thousand dollars. I'll check with the little wizards with the computers who figure out the lease payments and get back to you."

Wizards? Computers? Golly. I felt intensely threatened. To make sure I hadn't bollixed up the numbers, I asked what interest rate she was using.

"Nine point one four," she said. "That works out to a money factor of thirty-eight."

True enough. As you recall, the money factor equals half the monthly interest rate. .0914 per year = .0076166 per month, divided by 2 = .0038083. Or, .0914 divided by 24 = .0038083.

Interest or Lease Charges

Okay, we found something peculiar, maybe even a little fishy: According to one set of Lorna's numbers, we should pay off $6945 in monthly depreciation payments of $144.69. According to Lorna, however, we are paying $171.70 monthly depreciation. Plus $75.39 in interest. How does that number check out?

To generate the interest payment, we take the total money subject to lease charges, or capitalized cost plus residual value, and multiply it by the money factor.

$$
\begin{array}{r}
12815 \\
+\ 5870 \\
\hline
18685 \\
\times \qquad .0038 \\
\hline
71.0003 \text{ or } 71.00
\end{array}
$$

There's something a little strange about the interest payment, too. At $75.39, it's $4.39 too much. Where do these discrepancies come from?

Three Possibilities

1. BankLease may be using a higher capitalized cost.

Plugging a capitalized cost of $14,090 into the basic lease payment calculation yields a depreciation payment of $171.25, an interest payment of $75.85 and a lease payment of $247.10. After adding back the $600 rebate, the sell price would be $14,690.

Would BankLease quote a sell price of $13,415 while actually charging $14,690?

Maybe. Some lenders do this and legitimize it through semantics. The dealer cost of the car becomes "selling price." A chosen markup, from $1,000 to, in one case I've seen, $1,700, is called "dealer prep," or "acquisition fee." This second amount is added to the "selling price" to reach the capitalized, or acquisition cost on which the lease payment is based. And the figures are not revealed in your lease contract. They occur on the lessor/dealer worksheets.

2. BankLease's computer program may lower the residual when calculating depreciation and jack it up when computing interest.

If so, $4574 would be used to calculate depreciation and $7024 to calculate interest.

How do we arrive at $7024?

By reversing the operation which yields the interest payment: the same way you solve for the principal on a loan.

Dividing the interest payment Lorna quoted, $75.39, by the money factor of .0038 gives $19,839.47. Rounding off the pennies then subtracting the stated acquisition cost gives the residual: $19,839 − 12,815 = $7,024.

This possibility would yield the depreciation and interest payment amounts that Lorna quoted. As a bonus, it makes everything slightly unreal, and, you might say, post-modern. Simply charging a higher price could become unpleasantly real if a customer complained in the Consumer Corner of the local news. So I have a suspicion that calculating a lease payment with two different residual values is the true function of the Little Wizards and their computer.

3. BankLease may simply use a lower residual all the way around.

To figure out what that number may be we need a starting point. To find one (a) use a financial calculator to solve for residual value by keying in the payment. Or (b) figure out how much money the bank must make in order for the deal to make sense.

Assuming we don't have a financial calculator, doing "b" is easy. We simply compare earnings from two uses of the bank's money and come up with an amount we might call the "minimum acceptable profit"—because if the bank made less, they'd have no reason to lease cars.

If you borrowed $12,815 to buy the car, what would the bank earn in interest?

The going rate we've been using is 10.5% (in 1990); the 48 month factor for it is .0256.

Multiply 12,815 by .0256 to get the monthly payment for a 48 month loan: $328.06.

To get the total of the payments, multiply 328.06 by 48: which comes to $15,746.88 or $15,747. Interest earned by the bank is $15,747 − $12,815 = $2,932.

Now total up the lease payments: 247.09 × 48 = $11,860.32, or $11,860.

Subtract that amount from what the bank would make on the installment loan: $15,747 − $11,860 = $3,887. Therefore, to match the earnings on the loan, the bank would need $3,887 from the Taurus.

Now, let's plug this figure, $3,887, into the basic method of payment calculation. A $12,815 acquisition cost, $3,887 residual, 9.14% lease rate, and a .0038 money factor yield a 48 month lease payment of $249.46 a month.

We are in the ballpark, are we not?

Adding $100 to the residual brings us to $3,987 and yields a payment of $247.77. Now we've left the ballpark and are right next door. After a few more tries, a residual of $4,034 gave me a lease payment of $247.10. Eureka.

In the end, of course, it's just money: more money than the stated terms of the deal should warrant. And BankLease's computer may simply be adding a large ($1,507 divided by 48) administrative fee to each payment.

But—and here's the point of going through all these calculations—no matter how their computer calculates payments, we can state that *BankLease's deal is based on an effective residual value of $4,034.*

Question: If selling price or residual value are different than stated, is somebody lying?

Well, not exactly. You see, the lender/lessor can simply say, "We told you the price and the residual value. But we don't use them to compute the payment. We use something else."

That something else might be a fee of some sort added to the selling price to provide a different capitalized cost. Or a fee divided by 48 and added to the payment.

With the residual value, they could say something like this: "Well, $5,870 *is* the residual value. But what we use to compute payment is the *estimated future wholesale value*."

BankLease's deal shows in detail how the official residual value amount may function as your guaranteed buyout but differ considerably from what I'll call the real residual: the effective amount used to compute the lease payment.

Why is it done this way? To allow the lender to make as much money as possible on "big" deals, while at the same time covering itself on average deals.

Lease profits come mainly from the money brought in by selling cars turned in when leases expire. But it's almost impossible to estimate what these cars will actually bring in, because the spread in the retail prices of used cars of the same make and model is enormous, as much as $3,000.

Most cars, of course, will be average. The sensible thing to do to, then, is to base the lease payment on an estimate of a car's wholesale value in average condition. Such a payment is designed to bring in enough money so that the bank can sell most cars quickly, at wholesale prices, and still make an acceptable profit.

However, the possibility of selling a nice car for a nice, fat retail price—thousands over the wholesale price—always exists. The lessor does not want to let that fat price and that big, fat potential profit get away.

So your guaranteed buyout will be set on the assumption that your car will be fairly nice when you turn it in. It will be set at a price the lessor hopes to receive for a nice car, not the one it must receive to make a profit.

As a result, if you want the car, you pay the piper.

Not only that, but if you have a nice, clean, low mileage car, it will not be easy for you to make money by selling it yourself. Your nut, your payoff to the lessor, will be high. Thus the lender has a better chance of getting back that nice, clean car. And a better chance of taking the profit.

Lorna Spills the Beans

As I was cogitating about all this, time was going by and Lorna hadn't got back to me with an answer from the Little Wizards. This was the first time she had failed to call back when she said she would. Finally, I called her.

I said the buyout was too high for the payment, and vice-versa, then asked what was going on.

Again, she began comparing leasing to buying, and, again, I said that I understood all that.

Again, she said that leasing couldn't be calculated on an APR basis, and, again, I said I was using the depreciation basis.

Then I asked what the Wizards had told her.

She said, "Huh?"

I reminded her that she was going to ask the guys with the computers why the buyout was too high.

Now, she remembered. In fact, she did go to see the Wizards. But they hadn't got back to her. And now (she fussed around with something on her desk for a moment) now she couldn't find my file.

Never before had Lorna failed to find my file.

I did a little dance. I told her how helpful she was, how nice it was to deal with her, what a great deal BankLease offered, how much I wanted the car—but. But I had to have—absolutely had to have—the answers to these questions. (Remember that; it's an easy dance to learn.)

Then she said, "Oh, now I remember. There was a difference of a thousand dollars on the buyout."

"It was more than that," I said.

"No, I think it was a thousand. Let me go check."

She put me on hold and went off once more to visit the Wizards.

When she returned, she apologized all over the place and told me how embarrassed she was that she had forgotten about this. However, now she had the answer. The reason why things didn't jibe was, as she put it:

"The fact of the matter is that the computer added a thousand dollars in programmed profit structure. And that," she said, "accounts for the difference."

"A thousand where? In the payments, or the buyout?"

"In the overall," she said. "It's part of the computer program."

I asked if it could be negotiated out of the program.

No, she told me, it couldn't.

And there you have it, a wonderful, truly modern explanation of hidden charges: ". . . programmed profit structure."

Profit is no longer part of the price, like your boring, old-fashioned, run-of-the-mill type profit. Now, profit is part of the program. Where you cannot see it unless you know how to look.

How Many Beans Are We Talking about Here?

Had Lorna said the residual was $4,034, I would have wanted the option to buy the car at the end of the lease for $4,034. But as we saw, the bank wants to reserve potential profit for itself. How much is that potential? How does the bank make out on a lease as compared to a buy?

Here are some approximate numbers. They don't take selling costs into account, but if the bank either wholesales the car or sells it to you, those costs will be very low.

As noted, lending you $12,815 for 48 months at 10.5% would earn the bank $2,932 in interest.

Leasing you the Taurus at $75 over its cost would require an investment of $12,740. You pay $247.09 forty-eight times for a total of $11,860.32. Let's suppose that the sale of the four-year-old Taurus will bring from $3,200 to $5,870.

If the car brings $3,200, the total revenue is $15,060: the bank makes $2,320, about $600 less than it would on the loan.

If the car brings $4,000, the approximate residual, the total is $15,860. The bank makes $3,045, about $100 more than on the loan.

If the car brings $5,000, the total is 16,860, for a $4,120 return: an increase of almost $1,200 over the profit on the loan.

If you buy the car for $5,870, the total is $17,730. The return is $4,990 — more than $2,000 over the earnings on the loan.

This is why banks accept the extra risk of leasing.

What Does All This Mean to You?

If you understand the inner workings of the deal, including the lessor's profit expectations, you better understand the spread or range within which you may be able to negotiate both the monthly payment and the lease end purchase price.

Was BankLease's Deal a Good Deal? And How Can You Tell?

The payments we have compared to BankLease's have been all over the lot: $3 lower, $10 lower, $18 lower. Given that, and given the various methods of payment calculation, how would you decide whether or not you had a good deal going?

You would make the comparisons a little differently. We have been concerned mostly with the internal consistency of BankLease's arithmetic; you would be concerned with the market-place. It is the local marketplace which ultimately determines a good deal, not arithmetical consistency. For example, you would:

Go back to cost. With finance charges included it was $13,451. Round it off: $13,450.

Get a realistic sell price. Add $400: $13,850

Subtract the rebate of $600: $13,250.

Find out the manufacturer's estimate of residual value. In this case it's $5,697. Use that.

Determine the low average lease rate in your market. Here, 10%. (1990)

Inflate your price a little, since so many lenders do. Here we'll do it by adding a bank fee of $200, bringing the acquisition cost to $13,450. Calculate the lease payment, using the depreciation method. With the money factor for 10 per-

cent rounded up to .0042, the payment is $241.93. This is
your basic good deal.

Now raise the residual value factor by 3 or 4 percent. In
this case, that means 40%, and a residual value of $6,330.
Calculate a payment using this residual: it is $231.41. This
is your super deal.

Now split the difference. Add $5.50 to the super deal and
you have $236.91. This is your very good deal.

Are you likely to find the super deal? No, not in the Philly
area at the time of this writing: I called around. But in the
East Babbitt area you could have found a deal that good.
And in your area right now, it may be possible, so be aware
of it. A lender/lessor new in the market, looking for business,
might offer a deal that good.

Calculate a third payment using the method of the manufacturer's lease program. Find out what it is at a car store.
Here, with our present acquisition cost of $13,250, it would
be $246.72.

Shop. Look for $236—$237 a month before taxes while
being aware that it may be hard to find. Keep in mind that
anything between $240 and $245 will be pretty good. And
when you started shopping, you would let the salespeople
know that you had in mind a deal around $230—$231.
Later on, I'll tell you exactly how to let them know what
you have in mind.

BankLease's deal, then, despite the discrepancies, despite
the fact that it's terrific rate and selling price made the image much better than the reality, was still not really that
bad. It was a little high, but not a killer. And it could probably be beaten.

*Because the deal wasn't bad and probably could be beaten,
it would provide an extremely powerful bargaining tool, a bar-*

gaining tool so good we would probably have an easy time of it if we actually were out to lease the Taurus.

We'd simply go back to Skinny Tie and tell him we'd like to do business with him. But we'd been told that we could lease the car for $231 a month. So . . . what could he do for us?

And if you lived in an area where car stores were scarce and all run by folks who think discounts are a Communist plot, you could do BankLease's deal and not get murdered. And, despite what Lorna said, when you got off the phone and went into the office, you might be able to talk them down a couple of dollars a month.

The Taurus is a lot of car for the kind of money we've been talking about. The low payments came from:

(a) early charts, giving high residual values

(b) a rebate

(c) a huge discount. We started with a large package discount of $500, we negotiated or assumed we did, a store discount of fourteen to fifteen hundred, and we used Ford's $600 rebate (a factory discount) as cash down.

THESE ARE THE KEYS TO GETTING A GOOD LEASE DEAL:

EARLY CHARTS AND BIG DISCOUNTS WHICH MAKE THE MSRP — AND THEREFORE THE RESIDUAL VALUE — HIGH IN RELATION TO THE CAPITALIZED COST.

A BAD DEAL AT A FORD STORE

Would it really be as easy as it seemed in the last couple of sections? There's a good chance it would, because all of it actually happened. Then again, perhaps not. In any case, I don't want to tell you it will be easy; I want to show you that you can do it whether it's easy or not. So instead of going back to see Skinny Tie (which I would have done in real life) I went to another Ford store.

Following my own advice, I went to a big one, close to home. And, even though I know what I'm doing, with this stuff, anyway, I got jerked around all over the place.

The store was P & L Motors, in a rapidly growing suburb of a big city. Because you can be sued for telling unpleasant truths, let me add that this is a fictional name; that Ford Motor Company does not own this store or any car store I mention, nor does Ford control their behavior; and that the things that happened at P & L happen at dealerships selling all brands of cars.

First, I called and talked to a saleswoman named Josie. She said she'd give me a great deal. I said that was what I wanted and that I'd ask for her when I came in. When I got there, Josie was busy. I took a stroll around the lot to look at the Tauruses.

And immediately noticed a little sticker on the back window of every car. It said that the dealer had added a protection package composed of rustproofing, paint sealant, and fabric guard. The price of this package was $600.

I peered up under the wheel wells of a couple of cars and found that rustproofing had been sprayed on all the cars.

Bingo! Red flag number one. If I had been in the market for a car, I would have left immediately. But since I was in the market for research, I looked over the Tauruses.

Nothing quite matched what I wanted. The closest was stock number D1516, a silver metallic number that had a power passenger seat and a couple of other options I wouldn't want enough to pay for. The car had a sticker price of $15,873. P & L's add-on package brought the total up to $16,473.

Inside the store, I found Josie. We went into her office and sat down. She asked if I had found anything I liked.

I mentioned D1516 and said it was close, but had more options than I needed and it cost too much.

"Don't worry about that," said Josie. "We'll work out a nice payment for you."

"A nice payment?" What does this nice payment do? Say "please," and "thank you," and keep in mind the feelings of others? Nice? In a car store four hundred long, cold miles from this place I had learned that very phrase. And many others Josie used. All over the land, the same phrases are said in the same tones of reassurance.

Next, I asked about the dealer-added protection—or "pro"—package, saying I didn't want it and wasn't going to pay a nickel for it.

"Don't worry about it," said Josie. "I'll get it for you for free."

What a deal, right?

Wrong. So I kept complaining about it and said I wanted a car without the package. Josie said that would be impossible. The owner put the protection package on every car as soon as it came off the truck.

"He's a thickheaded, old-fashioned German," she said. The owner's inner nature and ethnic heritage had little to do with the rustproofing package. Josie was using the "it's-you-and-me-against-the-bad-guys" ploy. I was supposed to feel that she was my ally against the horrible old owner.

Then she told me again not to worry about the protection package, because she knew she could get it for me for free.

"I got the manager to give it to my last customers," she said.

What a gal, right? Wrong. This is an apparent discount of $600 that represents around $200 in hard dollars. That's not much on an Escort and nothing on a $16,000 Taurus.

So I changed the subject and asked how much a lease payment would be on the silver Taurus that listed for fifteen eight. Josie didn't like that subject, so she changed the subject herself. She asked what car it was.

I said it was the silver Taurus two cars in from the fence.

She asked if I was sure.

Was I sure?

With her question, Josie was trying to do two things. One, introduce doubt into my mind, plant the idea that I might be wrong. Two, take control of the conversation by forcing me to answer silly questions. And the first objective of that control was to steer me away from the subject of money till Josie had found out more about me.

"Let me go get the stock number and the invoice," she said. "That way, we'll know what we're talking about."

She went away and was gone a long time.

When she came back, she had an invoice, or, more accurately, part of an invoice. The outer and bottom edges, which bear the cost figures, had been folded under, then a copy made of the remainder, which showed only the retail figures.

Written by hand on the invoice was the stock number, D1516.

I glanced at it and handed it back to her.

"This is the wrong invoice," I said.

"No, no," says Josie. She is sure it's the right one. She points out the stock number.

I point out the price. List price on the invoice—without

dealer addenda—was $16,269, after an options discount of $400. But list price on the car's window sticker was $15,873, after an options discount of $500. Josie was showing me a fake invoice, hoping I hadn't paid much attention to the window sticker.

Josie said I must be mistaken, she was sure this was the right invoice: here was the stock number and everything.

I repeated the point about the price and pointed out the difference in the Ford package discounts.

We argued about this for a few minutes. Josie kept repeating that it must be the right invoice because it had the same stock number on it.

Note that we actually argued about this.

Finally, I told her to go look at the car. She went away again. When she came back she was full of apologies. She blamed the mistake on the office staff.

"The girl," she said, "must have put the stock number on the wrong invoice."

The girl hadn't done any such thing. The VIN numbers (serial numbers) on both invoices had been the same. The one Josie showed me was a fake.

Look closely at and remember what is written on the window sticker of the car you want. Burn those numbers into your brain. Window stickers come from the factory and it is against the law to alter or leave them off the automobile.

After Josie got done apologizing for "the girl's" mistake, I asked again what it would cost per month to lease that car. Instead of answering, she changed the subject again, then asked me for the third or fourth time how much I could afford to pay per month.

I hadn't answered—and don't you answer—this question up till now. If the salesperson presses you for an answer, say:

"Afford? I can afford this car if I get a good deal, that's what I can afford."

But now, after the dealer addenda and the phony invoice, I had had enough. To be able to show you how this game works, I told Josie I could afford about $300 a month.

Then she asked me how long a lease I wanted. I told her four years.

"Oh," she said, looking concerned, "I think we're looking at five years, here."

No, I told her, I was interested in four years.

"Well, she said, "let me go have the manager put it on the computer and see what it comes to."

Away she went, again. When she returned, she was carrying a piece of computer paper. She handed it to me. The faint, dot matrix printing said:

Financial Plan For:
D1516
"B" EXECUTIVE LEASE
Payment schedule:
59 at $300.00 + tax
Cash required:

1st Pmt	$318.00
Sec Deposit	$518.00
License Fee	$80.00
Prepayment	$38.16
Tax on Prepay	$0.00
TOTAL	$954.16
Residual	$5000.00

That's it, verbatim. Computerized compost.

Consider: If I negotiated a $1,200 discount (leaving almost $800 for profit, since the markup on this car would be close to $2,000) and used Ford's cash rebate as a down payment, I could buy the car on a Ford Credit 10.9% sixty-month loan for $318.51 a month including tax. Josie was offering a lease payment the same as a buy payment—on a buy deal that was barely decent.

Consider: On a 48-month lease for a car like this, you pay about $2.50 more per month for every $100 in increased cost. At $15,873 plus, say, $300 for the pro package, this car listed for $847 more than BankLease's.

At $2.50 per hundred, that's 8.47 times $2.50 = $21.18. Adding that $21 to BankLease's $247 payment equals $268; $268 and change per month (before tax) for 48 months.

P & L, however was asking $300 for 60 months: $5,100 more than I needed to pay. Eventually, of course, Josie would have knocked that payment down by about $25 a month. And I would have paid only $3,600 more than necessary.

And, finally, consider: After years in the car business, I had never before seen the "prepayment" that popped up in P & L's "Financial Plan." Maybe it was what I had to pay to round off the numbers. More likely, it wasn't anything but a little rip-off added to a big rip-off. If it were a payment for something, it would have been taxed.

P & L's Price

Using charts from three different lenders and a lease rate of 10.2% (money factor of .00425) I couldn't make a 60-month lease payment on a $15,873 car with a $5,000 residual value come out to $300 a month. Not even at sticker price plus $600 for add-ons.

The best I could do, using the phony invoice price of $16,269 then adding $600 for the "protection package," and another $200 for a bank fee, was just under $295 a month.

The lease payment Josie handed me for a car that retailed at fifteen eight was based on a price of about seventeen three to seventeen four. How about that?

Now, how about this: Some dealerships follow a standard practice of basing the first quoted lease payment on sticker plus 5 to 10 percent. I had stumbled into one of them.

P & L's *Payment Strategy*

Josie and her boss followed a script that might be called "Kick 'em Then Kiss 'em While They're Crying." Here's how it goes. It may happen to you.

They whack me with the $318 payment. Thinking I can't afford the car, I feel humiliated, afraid, angry.

All of a sudden, Josie sees the light. The manager, that dirty dog (at this point, you see, it's her and me against the manager), forgot to take off the $600 for the dealer-added package. She goes back to him. And comes back with a payment reduced by, say, $12.72, to $305.28 a month.

"There, that's better, isn't it, Mike?"

No. I can only afford $300 a month, no higher.

Away she goes again and back she comes with another reduction. Say, $297.94, with a $42 "prepayment."

"There," she says, "I really had to fight for you, Mike. I mean, I stuck up for you so much that my manager got mad at me. But now he'll lease you the car for $297.94, and that includes taxes. That's a hell of a deal. A really nice payment for you, Mike. A really good deal. Here, give me your O.K. right down here before he changes his mind."

If I object, she'll tell me that the new payment was twenty a month less, a twelve-hundred-dollar discount. She not only got me the protection package for free, she got the manager to take off another six hundred dollars!

This new figure represents a 60-month pretax payment of

$281.08 and a price of about $16,200. In other words, sticker, plus add-ons, minus a $200 discount on the add-ons. And a profit of twenty-six hundred dollars or thereabouts.

The add-on package, whether a protection package or a prettification package (the "decor group"), will have a retail price around three times its cost. Both the package and the payment strategy are designed to make you think you are getting a major discount while you buy the lease at sticker or sticker plus.

And when the salesperson asks how much you can afford per month, this is the scene she is setting for you. Your role is Prize Sucker.

Psywar: The Strategy Behind Josie's Sales Technique

In support of the payment strategy is an attempt to confuse you, wear you out, and make you doubt yourself and your idea of a good deal. Here's how salespeople try to do it.

Every assertion you make is challenged. Every time you say something, the salesperson contradicts you — even if she fully intends to agree with you and apologize later. Then, after a little argument, the salesperson leaves to check on something — and is gone a long time. You sit and wait and stew. Then the salesperson returns with a document.

The meaningless arguments and the irritation and boredom of waiting are intended to drain your energy, to wear you down before beginning the negotiation for dollars.

The (slightly) more meaningful arguments, coupled with the documents — and computerized documents at that — are meant to instill doubt. The salesperson's message is: *I am in the business; I have the invoice* [but not the cost figures] *and I have the computer. You don't have any of that so you must be wrong, especially about your idea of a good deal.*

The theory is that once you begin to doubt yourself, you

begin to suspect that the salesperson is right. After all, she is in the business. Maybe you made a mistake somewhere. What comes next is the basic propaganda technique known as the Big Lie. In the car business, it's known as *hammering* you.

The salesperson will insist, over and over, that she and her manager are right, that you are getting a good deal, that if they could lease you the car for any less they would do it in a minute. After all, they are there to sell cars, aren't they? Doesn't that make sense? And business has been bad: they are desperate to sell cars. If there was any way they could do what you wanted, they'd do it without another word.

Now, according to the plan, the force of repetition brings you to feel that you must be very close to getting the best deal possible. And once you reach that stage, a small but dramatic drop in the payment (dramatic because it crosses a psychological threshold), say, from $300 a month to, say, $297.94 a month, will make you feel a surge of relief. You'll think, "There, I got it." And sign. And lose a bundle. In this case, $3,600.

The alternate scenario: they pound away at you as above, but get nowhere. They decide you're a tough cookie. Then, instead of dropping the payment, they suddenly realize they've made a horrible mistake. The girl in the office pushed the wrong button on the computer. The payment is right, $300 a month plus tax, but the term really should be 48 months, not 60.

You think, "I knew it." And sign. Since the payment is $25 per month over the reasonably good deal payment of $275, you'd lose a mere $1,200 over the course of the 48 months.

If you begin to feel yourself being worn down, if you sense the onset of fatigue and doubt, leave. Even if you want to do business at that store, don't do the deal when you feel tired and weak. Walk out and come back another day.

DEALING WITH SALESPEOPLE AND SALES TACTICS

Most salespeople are more subtle than Josie. It's unlikely that you'll encounter one who plays her game so aggressively, so go for broke. If you do, tell her as pleasantly as possible to cut the bull. Then tell her you already know you can lease the car you want for such and such a payment. And ask how much better she can do for you.

Keep your cool. Be logical and polite. And repeat yourself till you want to barf. All the people we've talked to — Skinny Tie, Lorna, and now Josie — have tried to avoid answering questions. Skinny Tie said he didn't know the answer. Lorna answered different questions and changed the subject. Josie changed the subject, started irrelevant arguments, then went away, leaving me to cool my heels.

These ploys are intended to control the flow of conversation and to withhold information. Ignore them. Ignore what you do not want to hear and repeat your statements and questions until the salesperson responds.

There is, however, one sales game you'll find very hard to ignore.

THE BALL

If you are looking for a mass-market car and the salesperson thinks that you're shopping around for prices, you may get a response that knocks your socks off. You may get *balled*.

There's not much technique involved in balling. The salesperson simply says she will lease you the car for a price so low that you cannot get it for that price anywhere on earth.

The objective is to "take you out of the market," to prevent you from doing the deal anywhere else before you come back to see the salesperson who balled you. It gives her and the store one last shot at getting your business.

Balling is sometimes referred to as *highballing* and *lowballing*. The highball is an offer for your trade-in so far above its value that no one can match it. The lowball is an unmatchably low payment or sell price on the new car.

Whatever it's called, balling works. The main reason it works is that an unbelievable number of people try to hide the fact that they are shopping around. They tell salesman after salesman that he is the first salesman they've talked to. They say, "I just want your best price. Just gimme your best price."

Don't do this. It's a waste of everybody's time, including yours.

My best price is the most I can get out of you. If I have to give you a deal, it's the compromise I can make between you and the manager. If you've been shopping around, what I want to know is what payment will beat the other guys' and enable me to lease you the car right now, today. If you tell me what it is, I'll try to get it for you. And if I can't, I'll tell you what I can get for you.

But if you tell me I'm the first guy in a series, I'll quote you the unbeatable price. And the others will do the same.

The result of this is that customers shuffle from dealer to dealer, from ball to ball, from lie to lie. They become confused, frustrated, and angry. Then, very often, wherever they happen to be when they become so sick of it all that they can't stand it any longer, they do the deal. And end up not really knowing whether they got a good deal or not.

How to Dodge the Ball and Use It to Your Advantage

If you are shopping price from store to store, simply announce what you are doing. Don't ask for a "best" price or an "honest" price. Rarely will you get it. Salespeople learn, painfully, that when let out with an honest price, only one person in ten comes back.

Instead, tell the salesperson you're trying to beat a lease payment of x based on a sell price of y, whatever they happen to be. Make those numbers a bit lower than the best deal you think you can get. Then ask the salesperson if she can beat those numbers, and if so, by how much.

She will ask if you are ready to do the deal today. If you are, say so. If not, say so and tell her how many other prices you intend to collect. Handle this up front and swiftly.

If you say you're shopping around, she may quote a ball price to make sure you come back to her. You should—if you've done your homework—recognize immediately that the price/payment is impossibly low. Steel yourself: we all hate to admit that an impossibly low price is, in fact, impossible.

And then—this is a dramatic moment—once you spot a

ball price, recognize that you now have an edge. Check the price: have the salesperson go over everything with you.

When you're certain that the price is too low, accept the salesperson's offer and sign the deal. Hand over a deposit. Then sit back and enjoy the movie as the salesperson wriggles and jives and tries to explain why the manager won't accept that deal.

This movie should have a happy ending. For, once they've balled you, the salesperson and manager almost always abandon all hope for a big score. They accept the idea that you will get a good deal.

And you do get it. A manager who knows you've been shopping, believes you've been balled, and believes that you'll walk out of his store and lease the car somewhere else, feels extremely heavy pressure to take the deal away from the competition. That pressure is so heavy that, if they don't ball you, it may be wise to make them think someone else has.

To do this, tell the salesperson that someone has promised to lease you the car for the typical ball price: cost minus freight. (Look up cost in your cost/price book. Either leave out or subtract the freight.)

This price is so typical that almost everybody uses it. One reason is that freight runs $300 to $600, so a ball at cost minus freight will be well under a ball at cost minus, say, $200. Shoppers will return first to the store that quotes the lowest price.

The other reason it's widely used is that it provides a semibelievable excuse: "Oh, jeez, I'm sorry, I forgot the freight. They keep it separate, and I'm new on the job and . . ."

Cost less freight is so typical that most managers—in a competitive market—will recognize it immediately as a ball, as a price someone gave you so you would not lease the car elsewhere before coming back to see them.

To make it work to your advantage, simply assert that this happened. Use the price and payment at cost without freight as your first serious offer in the negotiation.

Exceptions

1. Cars in short supply. If you want a car for which demand outruns supply, saying that you've been offered a deal at the ball price probably won't mean much.
2. Cars with factory-subsidized leases. If you're shopping for a car with a factory-subsidized lease payment and stipulated term (number of months) the dealer will probably not be able to beat it *at that term*. But if you want a different term, everything is, as usual, up for negotiation. You should start negotiating with the same terms offered on the factory deal. You may or may not be able to get those terms (the factory is offering the subsidy to speed up the trade cycle) but that's where to start. See appendix B for the method of calculating the terms of the subsidized lease.

ATTITUDE AND YOUR ADVANTAGES

Negotiating is live, unscripted theater. There are, however, a few useful guidelines and a few helpful do's and don'ts. And there are moves and maneuvers you should be able to recognize. Some of them will be tried on you. First, let's discuss your attitude and advantages as a customer.

Attitude

Be reasonable. If you go out to get a deal at $300 over cost and wind up with one at $319, take it. Why drive around for days, suffer needless aggravation, not to mention wear and tear on your heart and stomach lining, all to save fifteen to fifty dollars on a ten- to thirty-thousand-dollar purchase?

Be nice. I don't mean be a wimp—if the salesman gets in your face, you get in his face—just be polite and friendly. Act as if you want him to like you because you want to sell him something. Which you do. You want to sell him the idea that giving you a good deal will be a quick and painless way for him to make a little money.

Furthermore, it may help you quite a bit later on if the salesperson's feelings about you are positive. He doesn't have to fall in love with you, just to think that you are a nice enough person to recommend him to someone else—if he is nice to you. What such feelings amount to is a salesperson who will go out of his way to help you later on, if you have trouble with your car. I once saw a salesman handle a service problem for a customer he didn't like. After the customer told him about the problem, the salesman looked him in the eye and said, "Do I look like a mechanic?" And turned around and walked away.

Don't play games. Don't try to talk big, don't act tough, and don't poor-mouth.

Allow yourself plenty of time—and take your time. Let the salesman play his games; let him go through his routine. Don't rush things. The more time he spends with you, the more he has to lose, so the more he'll want, and need, to make a deal with you.

Try to put yourself in the salesperson's shoes; understand his advantages over you and your advantages over him. The people who sell cars have a certain boldness or audacity.

They are not afraid to tell half-truths and outright lies—and not afraid to be caught at it. They know the numbers on the cars or can find them out easily. They have training and practice at running scams. And they have experience in high dollar negotiations.

All of that notwithstanding, you are in control of the salesperson's most potent tools. For salespeople use two things to make big scores: the customer's ignorance and the customer's emotions. If you have the handle on those things, the salesperson does not. Replace ignorance with knowledge and keep your emotions under control, and the slickest, most skillful salesperson on the planet will have little to work with.

And most of the salespeople you meet won't be all that slick. If they were, they wouldn't be selling cars to the public. They'd be selling guided missiles or six-hundred-dollar toilet seats to the government, working fewer hours, eating in much better restaurants, and making three times as much money.

So don't be intimidated.

And don't feel that you need to be hostile to keep the salesperson off balance. Hostility often doesn't work, and if it doesn't, you merely waste good will—and give the salesperson a motive to seek revenge, later.

There are no games, no tricks, and no techniques of negotiation that will give you the power that self-control and knowledge will give you. None.

Your Advantages Over Salespeople

Everybody in the store needs you more than you need them.

A lot more.

If they do not do your deal at your price, the salesperson loses the commission, the manager loses his commission, and the house loses its profit. No matter how small that commission or profit would have been, none of them can ever make it up. For there are no more you's.

There are, however, plenty of other cars at plenty of other stores. You do not lose the car. They lose and you don't.

And they know it.

Therefore, a salesperson would much rather give away most of the profit than lose a sale. A slice of bread is better than no loaf at all. (Always better for the salesperson; not always for the manager—that is, until the end of the month rolls around.)

To show you what I mean, at the East Babbitt Ford Store, a skinny little $200 deal would earn: a 25% commission on the profit, or $50; a $25 delivery fee or bonus; and done deal. Every done deal brought a salesperson closer to earning the monthly incentive bonuses, which came in varying amounts depending on the number of cars sold. After a certain number sold, the per car amount of the bonus went up. After so many more, it went up again. If a skinny deal on which I made very little money boosted me to a level where I received an extra $10 per car bonus, for, say, 15 cars sold, that skinny little deal would earn me not only the $75 but also an extra $150 in bonus money.

There's also a boost in morale and the very real possibility that the customer will send in a friend or two, resulting in a couple more deals. You figure it out. Who needs who? Do not feel that you are chiseling or wasting a salesperson's time by going after a good deal.

You Control the Money

This may seem obvious. Perhaps not so obvious is that you control it most powerfully after you've made a deposit.

When you make a written offer on a car, the offer is supposed to be accompanied by a deposit. If the deposit isn't there, the salesperson gets reamed. Behind the demand for a deposit is a theory: once you hand over cash, you hurdle the principal psychological barrier between you and the deal; when you hand over cash, you commit yourself to buying or leasing that car.

This is supposed to, and usually does, make it easier for the salesperson to "work" you, which means manipulate your emotions, and to "raise" (or "bump") you, which means persuade you to pay more. For once you have committed yourself, it is quite painful to be denied. But now the store, through its pricing power, can deny you the car. Your human need to avoid emotional pain makes you easier to manipulate.

Many customers, aware of this, hate to pay the deposit. But if you have control of yourself, the deposit gives you more power over them than they gain over you.

The moment you part with cash, both salesperson and manager become more confident that they'll make the deal. Even though they know they shouldn't, they begin to count their chickens; they begin spending the extra money your deal will put into their paychecks that month.

And now you have the power to take that money away from them. If that hurts them more than losing the car hurts you—if you are willing to give up the car, and your salesperson knows it—you gain an edge the moment you make a deposit.

The Walkout

And your edge in action is . . . the walkout. This is your ace of trumps, your killer move. It is simply the threat to leave the dealership without doing a deal. It comes in an infinite variety of shapes, forms, and intensities. And the great thing about it is (as the boss said of the lease payment) that they (salespeople and managers) can never figure it out. They never know for certain whether or not you mean it.

For it's always an ultimatum—but never really an ultimatum until you actually get into your car and drive away. Remember, when negotiating, you can agree with anything, promise anything, threaten anything, and then take it all back in the next breath. You can walk all the way to the door (the salesman will probably follow you) then turn around suddenly and say, "Hey, I like this place. Why can't I get a fair deal here?"

Or you can merely glance at your watch and stir restlessly in your chair. The salesperson will be paying close attention to your body language. Get restless and she will start to worry.

Or, if seated, you can stand up. When a customer stands without explanation, the first thing that flashes through a salesperson's mind is, "Oh, no. He's leaving. What did I do wrong?"

And if you walk away from the desk and wander out into the showroom, hearts will stop. For everybody in the place thinks that a customer not under complete control is a customer ready to bolt out the door. With you wandering around, even the tough-as-nails managers will feel as if the sky is falling.

After you've made the deposit, you don't even have to move. Just mutter: "I dunno. We can't seem to get anywhere. Maybe you should give my money back."

Give back? Give back money? Every fiber of your salesperson's being will scream with pain. You get the idea. The variations are endless. But employ them judiciously; don't bluff too often.

The Salesperson's Countermoves: "Rational" Arguments

People have heard that salespeople will not argue with them. "Win the argument, lose the sale," the saying goes. But as Josie was kind enough to show us, this ain't necessarily so.

In fact, a large part of a salesperson's skill consists of the ability to provide convincing, nonthreatening reasons why everything you say is wrong. The argument cannot become sharp enough to offend you, but because the salesperson is fighting information that you've gathered from God only knows where, some form of argument must be carried on. Here are some of the points your salesperson may try to argue and win:

The salesperson is in the business and has the facts; neither you nor anyone you have talked to really knows anything. We have seen this one in action.

Even if you do have some knowledge, you have unknowingly made a mistake. For example, if you have a legitimate payment quote, and it's an O.K. deal, your salesman will not want to hear about it. So he may try to discredit it by saying it's based on a residual value from charts that are too old, or charts from the wrong lender.

Do this: When somebody quotes you a lease payment, write down all the relevant details, including name of the lender, month of the residual value charts, the factor—or percentage of MSRP—being used to figure the residual, and the residual value dollar amount. With this information, you can cross-check what the next salesperson tells you.

Or the salesperson may claim that your price or payment

is based on the wrong car, a car with a smaller engine or fewer options.

Write things down. For if you do happen to get a price quoted on a car with a couple hundred dollars' fewer options than you want—which happens frequently—you'll drive yourself crazy trying to match or beat it on a car that has all the options.

If you have a trade: the salesperson would pay you exactly what you want for it—except. Except that, unbeknownst to you, your car is one of those that is famous for needing repairs to the camshaft, or the constant velocity joints, or the computer controlled bivalvic nosewiper. And that just happens to be a five-hundred-dollar repair, so . . .

This argument sometimes begins with a neat ploy, a game we might call Whatever You Want, I'll Give You More. If you want $3,000 for your car, the salesperson says, "Gee. I might be able to get you close to four. Could we do business?"

Ooooh, ooooh, ooooh, could we ever! This is an appeal to your pride and greed. The object is to stir up your emotions so the salesperson can manipulate them, then draw from you an offer and deposit: a commitment to lease the car.

Once that's done, the salesperson begins pointing out a few of the thousand and one defects of your car, gradually hacking away at the trade allowance. All the while, she blames the manager. The manager says it needs new paint. The manager says the transmission is bad. The manager says the tire sidewalls are cracked. The manager says the window glass is hard to see through, etc., etc. As did Josie, the salesperson will blame anything and anyone she can think of. She agrees with you, absolutely. But you must be wrong, because everyone else says so.

With leasing, you are sometimes told flat out that you

don't know what you are talking about. As with Lorna's explanation, "Leasing doesn't work that way." Or, "There is no price when you lease." How would you respond to the last statement?

You would say, "Sell price, minus cash down, minus trade equity, plus lender fees, plus cash owed on trade equals capitalized cost." Right?

Agreement

Agreement about important things occurs in the form of a question. If you say your trade-in is worth three thousand and the salesman agrees with you, he'll say something like: "What if it is? If I could get you the three thousand, would you lease the car today?"

The form of that question reveals the template used to structure negotiations: "If I could . . . would you?" If I could [do whatever it is you want] would you [take the car].

A good salesperson makes as few statements as possible. The fewer the statements, the less information revealed. And the fewer lies told. Notice that the salesman did not say, "I'll get you three thousand. . . ."

The Salesperson's Countermoves: Emotional Games

Those are a few of the more common "rational" sales games.

Here are some of the emotional ones. I've listed them as do's and don'ts, mostly don'ts.

1. Don't be frightened by a payment quote way over sticker. No matter when it occurs in the deal, it's part of the "take away close." It's supposed to frighten you, to loosen up your emotions so the salesperson can calm you, soothe you, and then smooth you into paying a bunch.

2. Don't believe that salespeople who appear slow, steady, calm, and polite are therefore trustworthy. This is a common belief. It is also an expensive belief.

3. Don't believe that young, inexperienced, or clumsy salespeople will be nicer to you, will help you out, or will be unable to lie effectively. This is an even more common belief.

Managers control inexperienced salespeople very closely. They use youth and inexperience as a cover for flagrant lies, gambling that such people will sound truthful when they say that there's only $1,000 markup on an $19,000 car, or something equally ridiculous. For youth and inexperience create the illusion of innocence.

On top of that, managers will rarely allow new salespeople to sell a car as cheaply as experienced ones. The neophyte is being trained, and no one trains people to sell cars, or anything else, by giving away money. Once they know how to sell, or so goes the theory, they will give away money only when they have to.

4. Don't trust a salesperson who appears to be your "brother," your "sister," your "soulmate," your "homie," or your "paisan." Someone who shares your gender, your ethnic heritage, your deepest interests, or your age group and its most profound life experiences will grease you up and down and all over with this sharing. But if you allow yourself to be affected by it, the salesperson will take a larger share of your money.

5. Don't trust a salesperson because he or she is cute and acts as if he or she likes you, and might, if you play your cards right, do certain enjoyable things with you. The biggest score made while I was at the Ford store came from a customer who believed this; it is the most expensive belief of all.

6. Do be careful when you are given freebies or when the salesperson agrees with you too easily. Nothing is free. Either you've already been taken for a bundle, or, perhaps,

the salesperson is setting you up for the sneakiest scam of all: the phony payment scam.

The Phony Payment Scam

This is when winning on price equals losing on payments. The salesperson simply agrees to lease you the car at the price you want, then writes in a payment that is five, ten, or fifteen dollars a month too high. If you catch him, it's an honest mistake. He looked at the wrong chart. Or he added in life, accident, and health insurance, which everybody wants, because something, God forbid, but something could happen to you. . . . But if you don't want it, he'll just take it right out. If you don't catch him, everybody's happy. Do not expect to be rescued from the phony payment scam by seeing the price on the contract. The vast majority of lease contracts contain nothing remotely resembling a price. And do not expect to be rescued by the factory's credit company, as was my truck customer. Even if you've been charged over sticker, all a salesperson has to do to turn phony payments into sincere payments is throw in a free protection package on a "special."

Who could resist? Protection from this, protection from that, all for free? Nobody could resist. Then, on the dealership's leasing worksheet, the manager would price the protection package at whatever figure was needed to bring the cost of the vehicle back down to sticker price. If I had thought of that, I could have sacrificed $150 of profit to retain $350.

Do the games and scams never end?

Frankly, no. But don't worry. You can handle most of them simply by doing your homework. As for the rest, take a lesson from the salesperson's training manual.

Salespeople are taught that customers lie continually. Since these lies are all part of a game, however, they should never cause the reaction they would in everyday life. Instead, they should go in one ear and out the other.

You do the same. Politely ignore everything the salesperson says except what you need to hear. When he tells you which button controls the power wingding, pay attention. When he tells you what residual value and lease rate he's using, pay attention. When he explains a clause in the contract, pay attention. When he tells you that your price is way off base and gives you seven reasons why, think about a nice day at the beach.

And finally: Do expect to be treated well.

If you are not, if the salesperson is too pushy, or refuses to answer your questions, but you feel she has potential, tell her about it. If she doesn't improve, or you feel she cannot improve, leave. Salespeople are taught to put themselves into your shoes and to treat you as they would like to be treated. If they cannot master that lesson, they don't deserve your business.

The Car: That Sweet Object of Desire

Of all the emotional sales aids, the one carrying the greatest charge of emotion is, of course, the car itself.

A salesperson's goal is to increase your desire for the car and to heighten your sense of urgency, till everything in you is screaming, "I want it and I want it *now.*" So she will be sure to point out that the car is, indeed, a many splendored thing. She will, or is supposed to, demonstrate every feature and option that makes the car valuable. The purpose is to create in your mind a concrete picture of tremendous value. For people do not do deals when they are thinking about the money they are going to spend. They do deals when they are thinking about what they are going to get. The salesperson wants to take your mind off the deal for dollars and lock it onto the deal for value.

You can use the entire routine to gain information.

· Make sure the car has the options you want—and the options the sticker says it has. Find out where all the controls are and how they work.
· As the salesperson is showing you various features, ask about how completely and how long they are covered by the warranty. Don't be shy about asking "dumb" questions. Nobody expects you to know everything about the new car.
· Check carefully for dents and scratches. Also check for misaligned body panels. Everything should look like it fits together properly. Open and close all the doors. Make sure they close easily. If they don't now, they probably never will.
· Inside the car, check for misaligned door and headliner upholstery panels. If the seams are crooked, or the pieces of cloth appear to have been put on in the dark, you're looking at a wrong car. Find another one. And if it's night, be sure to have the car pulled into the garage—the brightly lit garage. If the garage is dim, return and inspect the car during the day.
· Read the window sticker. Read it thoroughly. Check the options carefully. Talk about it, if talking helps you remember. *Burn the MSRP, factory discount, and sticker price into your brain!* Remember, a price and package discount discrepancy was how I spotted Josie's phony invoice.
· What you can't use this routine for is to talk in any

meaningful way about price or payments. Many people try, but it's a waste of time.

THE TEST DRIVE

In most stores in most areas, the test drive is an important part of the pageant of splendors: a selling tool. The salesperson wants you to feel the difference between the new car and your old rattletrap. She wants you to smell that new car smell. She wants you to feel that smooth, tight, quiet new car ride.

When driving the car, make sure everything fits and works. Make sure it accelerates, shifts, and handles properly. That the radio works, the heater works, the air works, all the power doodads work, the windshield wipers and squirters work, and so on.

Not only does this give you a chance to check out the car, but, in stores where test drives are seen as selling tools, it also makes it easier for your salesperson to handle his or her boss during the deal.

This is important. The salesperson will be trying to manipulate both you and the manager at the same time. No matter how much the salesperson wants to give you the deal you're asking for, his boss will be telling him to sell you the house deal. Your driving the car will make it much easier for him to sell the boss your deal.

If the manager discovers that you didn't drive it—as he probably will—he'll get angry. And then he'll make an assumption. He will assume that you are making a low offer because the salesperson did not do his job. He will assume the salesperson failed to whet your appetite for the car. He won't take your low offer very seriously, assuming you would offer more had your desire been properly tweaked.

Therefore, he may very possibly reject a deal he would otherwise take.

O.K., you're driving. Suppose the engine, transmission, axles, or some other part of the drivetrain makes funny noises? By "funny," I mean grinding, clicking, ticking, howling, or moaning noises.

Forget it. Find another one.

Suppose it runs rough? This is a judgment call. If you think the engine is running rough because of dirty spark plugs, or some other minor problem, it's probably worthwhile to make a contingency deal.

This means that you include a note on the purchase order form saying that the deal is contingent upon the car running smoothly (or other problem being solved) when you test drive it again before taking delivery.

Before taking delivery. Come back in a day or two and drive it. If it still doesn't run right, find another one. Or cancel the deal and get your deposit back. Don't take a car that the dealer has failed to fix on the first try.

Don't take it even if you've already signed the lease contract.

The F & I Guy, or business manager, who handles financing, life, accident and health insurance, and, increasingly, the sale of after-sale items like rustproofing, paint gloss, etc., will try to talk you into signing the contract ahead of time. Don't do that, either.

Remember, no matter how many times a salesperson or a manager says, "You bought it, pal [or honey]," you can always cancel the deal until you actually drive that car off the lot. You say, "I don't want the car. Give me my money back."

Dealing with Irrational Managers

There is one thing that can screw up the works and be impossible to recognize while it's happening: certain managers at certain times will not accept reasonable deals, let alone good ones. Behind the refusal lies anger, ego, or fear.

Sometimes a salesperson will do something that gets the manager pissed off. Then, amazing as it may seem, the manager may make the salesperson pay for her mistake by refusing a deal he'd normally take in a minute.

Sometimes the manager is just whacked out. One of our guys was a Big Dude. On occasion, he'd decide the profit on a deal, although quite reasonable, wasn't big enough for the size of his Dudedom. And, bang, he'd turn it down. Wasting the salesman's time, the customer's time, and denying the house a deal.

And some managers simply don't have the self-confidence to take a deal when, as they say, it's all the way down to the bone. Put another way: when profit is so slim that the reason may have to be explained to the owner. Other managers, however, will take that kind of deal.

Try to go around a problem manager, not through him. If you are offering a small but reasonable profit and cannot get your deal accepted, try the following steps.

1. Ask the salesperson what the manager's problem is. She may know, and may tell you, for a salesperson's lot in life consists of trying to manipulate the manager at the same time she's trying to manipulate you.

2. Get another manager involved with the deal. If your salesperson doesn't think of this, tell her about it. Tell her to check with another manager, to get a second opinion on the value of your trade or the acceptability of the profit. This may require either delicate diplomacy or consider-

able courage. If the salesperson feels she can't handle it, she may suggest that you try your third option.

3. Leave and come back another day when another manager is available.

Sometimes these moves work. They've worked for me. But "come back another day" can also work as a ploy. You walk out. Then you come back, expecting a better deal. But all you can get is the same deal. The salesperson has had you put in more time; she's trying to wear you down.

Ask about this before agreeing to the tactic. And before you do come back, call the store. Make sure that the manager who is supposed to make you a better deal is there — and will still be there when you arrive.

NEGOTIATING
THE LEASE

Now that we have an overall sense of the balance of power beween you and salespeople, let's talk in detail about negotiating the price and lease payment. First we'll discuss a "clean" deal, that is, without a trade, and then on a deal where you trade in your old car.

Either way, you should prepare by "crunching the numbers." That is, you should work out a series of lease payments from about 10% below cost to 10% above sticker. If you're not trading in, figure out a set of lease payments something like this:

1. 10 percent under cost (without pack). (Use this if the house starts high and seems reluctant to deal.)
2. The ball price: cost without freight.
3. Cost plus half the freight.
4. Cost with freight but without pack.
5. Cost plus $100 for the pack, or dealer cost.

6. Cost plus pack plus a little profit.
7. A little more profit and a little more: a couple of haggle prices, up to the amount you are willing to pay.
8. Cost plus a lot of profit.
9. Sticker price.
10. Sticker plus 10 percent.

Doing this may take an hour or more, but it is eminently worth the time and trouble. Knowing these numbers will enable you to have a clear picture of the deal for dollars all the way through. You will have a clear idea of:

· where you are and where you are going
· where the house offer is in relation to yours
· when to stop and dig in your heels
· the dynamics of the negotiation; that is, the motive behind their offers to you. Are they dropping price fast to where you want to be? Or are they trying to hang on to every last penny of profit?

I believe, too, that doing the numbers ahead of time will make it easier for you to maintain your self-confidence. They'll provide clear boundaries and road signs for you, in case the salesperson creates a blizzard of B.S.

THE PURCHASE ORDER FORM

When you sit down at the salesperson's desk, he or she will produce the purchase order or purchase offer form. It is not a contract; it's more like a letter of agreement or letter of intent. When signed by the manager, however, it tends to bind the store. So, when the deal is done, make sure the manager signs that form. If he doesn't (at a few stores, not all) you leave yourself open to the "bump on delivery." In this nasty little scam, you're told you have a deal. But when you come in to take delivery, you find that they have discovered a mistake. They tell you, sorry, but they undercharged you. You must pay more or you cannot have the car.

What to Have Written on the Purchase Order Form

The salesperson will write down your name, address, and phone number. He will probably write down a list of the car's equipment, and, perhaps, the sticker price.

He may, however, skip the price and write down only a lease payment. It will probably be expressed like this:

"Customer will lease for x months for \$$x$ per month plus tax [plus trade, if you have one]." That formula, "customer will lease for a certain number of months for a certain amount per month plus tax [and trade]," was the way I expressed 99 percent of the lease deals I wrote. Remember that formula. And realize that it opens your wallet for the salesperson.

What you actually want is for the purchase order form to recapitulate the payment calculation. It should say something like this:

"Customer will lease for _____ months based on a sell price of \$_____, minus cash or trade (if any), leaving a capitalized cost of \$_____, minus a residual value of \$_____, leaving a depreciation of \$_____, a depreciation payment of \$_____, and an interest payment of \$_____, based on an _____ percent interest rate and a money factor of _____, for a monthly lease payment of \$_____."

Resistance

Your salesperson isn't going to want to write all that stuff down, and may not even know how. If he doesn't know how, he is not going to want to ask the manager to do it. So you'll probably get a song and dance. He'll tell you you'll see it later, or you'll see it on the contract, or only the computer can produce that information.

If you hear anything like this, bring up Regulation M. Remind the salesperson that the information has to be on the form mandated by Regulation M, so why don't they get that form right now. Or get the contract if the form is on the contract, and start filling it out right now, as the deal is being done. Press for this, and you will get it. Not only are you entitled to all of this information simply by virtue of being the customer, but mentioning Regulation M will remind your salesperson that you are legally entitled to it as well.

THE TWO ROADS: TO DICKER OR NOT TO DICKER

What happens next depends on your approach. You must make a choice between the direct approach and the negotiation.

I tend to agree with people whose advice is: don't dicker. Simply announce the deal you want, push for it until you get it, and, if you don't get it, walk out.

The Direct Approach

Have the salesperson write the deal you want on the purchase order form in terms of price, capitalized cost, and payment. Sign it. Hand over ten or twenty bucks for the deposit. Make sure the salesperson understands that this is your offer, not a talking point. Tell him, this is it: this is as far as you go. Ignore his protestations.

But try not to be too abrupt. Sugarcoat your demands. Tell the salesperson that you want to do business with him and you are ready to do it right now, today. If he gets you your deal, it will be the quickest, easiest money he's ever made. That's the benefit you are selling the salesperson: quick, easy money; no sweat, no strain.

This will be meaningful, believe me. If the salesperson has any experience at all, he will have suffered through knockdown, drag-out deals where he made no more money than you are offering for a few minutes of pleasant chat.

You may, however, encounter resistance. After all, the shortest distance between two points is the route on which your salesperson makes the least money. So he will try to turn it into a negotiation.

Resistance to the Direct Approach

Resistance will first come in the form of asking you to justify your price. The salesperson will ask, "Where in the world did you get your figures?" His tone of voice will imply you got them from outer space.

Then, more seriously, either he will ask you to justify, that is, explain the rational basis for your price and your payment. Or he will assert that your price is impossible, that your figures are wrong.

Say that you've looked up the numbers—after all, anybody can look up the cost of a car. Then you figured out the deal you wanted. Then you went to a few places and checked: you shopped around. And you know you can lease the car for that price. If not here, then somewhere else. But you want it to be here. Because you like the place, or it's convenient for you, or because you heard they had good service.

Other Forms of Resistance

· If you have a trade, the salesperson may disagree with what you are asking for it. Say that you shopped it

around and got offered x, y, and z. You know you can
get what you're asking.

· If he agrees about the price of the car and the trade
allowance but argues with your payment, say that you
learned how to figure it out, then shopped around and
double-checked.

· He may imply you are fibbing about your trade by asking why you didn't take one of the other deals you were
offered. Tell him that you need a car to drive: you can't
sell the old one till you get a new one. And that's why
you're here, with him, trading in, offering him some
fast, easy money.

Give these answers once. If the salesman keeps pressing
for further justification, turn the tables on him. Start asking
him to justify his refusal to make the deal with you. Say,
politely, that you told him where you got your numbers,
and they sound like a good deal. Unless he can beat that
deal. Can he? If not, why not? Why can't he do better than
that for you?

Make him feel that refusing your offer will cause you to
lower it, not raise it.

Pound into the salesman's brain a few simple facts. One,
you know what you're doing. Two, you have faith in yourself
and your numbers. Three, you will not be moved: the only
deal you'll take is the one you've just stated. When he is
convinced of this, he'll start trying to convince the manager.

If the salesman refuses to be convinced, he's trying to get
around you, to circumvent the direct approach and force
you into a negotiation. Use the walkout. Start mild: move
around restlessly in your seat. Increase the intensity if necessary. The salesman will become convinced.

As you probably know, salespeople are not permitted to authorize deals. So now he'll take your deposit to the cashier and the purchase offer, or deal, to a manager. And now you will enter a form of negotiation whether you want to or not. For few managers will accept your offer without making a few counters of their own. To stay with the direct approach, you must cut this process short.

THE MANAGER'S COUNTEROFFER

The Direct Approach — Low Counter

If the counter is low, only a hundred or two above your offer, it usually means the manager has pretty much accepted the idea that you will get your deal, but he's duty bound, of course, to try for another buck or two.

Just say no. Start fussing around restlessly as if getting ready to leave. Push the purchase offer toward the salesman. Say, "That's it. That's my price. Get it for me, or we can't do any business." Repeat this till it either works, or you become certain it will not work. At that point, ask for your deposit back.

A salesman cannot give back a deposit. He has to talk to a manager and a manager has to sign your receipt before the cashier will take the cash or check out of the till. And managers do not return deposits on the first request. They send the salesperson back with another offer. In the case of a low initial counter, the next offer will probably be what you want.

If not, tell the salesperson it's still too high and you want your money back. After going away this time, he will return with your deal or your deposit.

The Direct Approach—High Counter

The manager may counter at a much higher price. For example, you offer two hundred fifty over cost and she counters at one hundred under sticker.

The manager is trying to stonewall you. Don't bother with discussion. Move immediately to the walkout. Tell the salesman that it looks like you can't do any business here and ask for your deposit back. He'll go back to his manager and explain that you won't budge, that you are asking for your money back, and that they have to return it to you or make your deal.

The Direct Approach—Medium Counter with Hammer

The manager's counter will be about halfway between sticker price and where you want to be. But with this offer, she will tell the salesperson to hammer you. The salesperson will say they simply cannot meet your figures. This new offer is the absolute lowest they can go without losing money on the deal. He will say it over and over, in a dozen different ways. And it will sound like the truth.

Don't be intimidated. Instead, tell him—politely—to prove it. Tell him you want to see the invoice—the part with the cost figures, not the retail figures. Give him these alternatives: you want the deal at your price, you want your deposit back, or you want to see the cost figures on the invoice showing why he can't meet your price.

They won't want to show you the invoice. So now you'll either get your deal or get your deposit back. And leave. If you do leave, but the place is convenient and has a good reputation, it may be worthwhile to come back the next day. Sometimes nothing short of walking out will convince a manager that you mean what you say.

When you return, ask your salesperson if his boss is going

to let him do some business and make a little money today. Remind him that it was his loss when you walked out—not yours—and blame it on the manager.

Incidentally, if the direct approach doesn't seem to work, and you decide to try negotiating, you might try this: Tear up the old purchase order. Right in front of your salesperson's nose. And ask for a new one.

When the salesperson asks with amazement what the hell you are doing, simply say that your previous offer was rejected, so it doesn't exist anymore. It is history. Then say, "If I have to jump through hoops to make a deal, I want a better one."

When he gets the new order form, write a new offer on it. Drop big time. Offer a thousand dollars less than your first offer. You don't want to begin negotiating with an offer that puts the house into profit.

If you do this, your salesperson will have a moment of true panic. He'll think, "Oh, man, this stupid manager just cost me a hundred bucks!" As they say in the car business: Believe me when I tell you. A customer pulled that trick on me once, and I was truly discombobulated.

NEGOTIATION: OFFER—COUNTEROFFER

Or, more accurately, counter, counter, counter, counter, till everybody's blue in the face.

If you decide to go with negotiation, fool around for a while with some very low offers. Offer them a payment based on a price that is at least a thousand dollars under dealer cost. Your salesperson will advise you to rejoin reality.

You Get Serious: Reality Is a Ball

Tell him the reality is: you want to pay the ball price, cost without freight, with the corresponding payment. Be very serious. You are no longer fooling around. This offer is not a talking point. This offer is written down on the purchase order. You sign it and you back it up with a deposit. You are not playing. You absolutely believe you can lease the car for this price because another salesperson told you so.

If the salesperson is sharp, she may ask you: if it was such a good deal, why didn't you take it? Tell her that this store is more convenient, or has a such a reputation for honesty, good deals, and good service, that you'd rather do the deal here. Use flattery whenever possible. They cannot disagree.

But don't be facetious. This is a serious offer. You believe you can lease the car for this price. Have the salesperson write it on the purchase order form. Sign it. Hand over a twenty dollar deposit. Remind your salesperson you have been shopping and you have been told you can lease the car for this price. Force her to take the offer to the manager. Then sit tight.

The Manager's Reaction to Your Offer at the Ball Price

In a competitive market for vehicles in good supply, most managers are quick to spot a ball price. And most of the time they handle it in a relatively straightforward fashion.

Believing that someone has promised you an impossible price, the manager will feel that his hands are pretty much tied. He'll figure his best bet is to explain to you that you've been offered a price below dealer cost, then offer you a very reasonable deal at a very small profit.

He will think this way because even a terrific bargain will be far higher than the ball price: the cost of the freight plus the pack plus the profit.

Thus, for him to make a profit of $200 on even a low-priced car, you will have to pay at least $600 more than you (supposedly) believe you have to pay. That's a lot of money.

And a nice profit of $400 to $1,500 is a lot more. So the manager will feel that it's not safe to try for a decent profit. He will fear that if he does, you'll leave. And probably not come back.

He believes that you will not come back even after you find out that the other price was a fake. "Bebacks"—people who walk out the door saying, "I'll be back"—very rarely come back. No matter why they leave, no matter why they say they'll be back.

So the manager may even send the salesperson back with the invoice, willing to try anything to convince you that the ball price is fraudulent and that his reasonable price, some $600 to $800 more, is honest.

This reasonable price should be very close to what you want—and maybe even better. It would not be unheard of to make a quick deal at $250 over dealer cost on a $14,000 to $16,000 car, whereas you had been willing to pay up to, say, $325 over.

Bargaining: An Overview of Moves and Countermoves

First of all, here are a couple of emergency tactics you can use if things get complicated and you start feeling a little confused. These tactics can be drawn out for as long as you need to regain your composure.

1. Tell the salesperson that her payment seems wrong; it seems too high for her price. Then ask her to show you each step in her calculations.

2. Tell her you feel sudden, serious doubts about leasing. Then ask to see the lease contract. Then start reading it. Ask about this clause or that clause. Since it would take a day or so to read and understand the average lease contract, this should give you plenty of time to pull yourself together.

A *Mystery Solved: What Do They Talk about When the Salesperson Goes Away?*

This is the most basic of dealership sales ploys. It gives you time to cool your heels; it makes you feel that something really important is going on: when the salesperson returns she will bring with her the results of a major deliberation.

What they are doing is talking about you. The salesperson tells the manager what you said and what she said. The manager then asks questions about you: how much money you make, what you drive now, why you are getting a new car, etc. He's trying to figure you out from afar, trying to decide what to do in order to get more money out of you. If he thinks of something, he suggests it to the salesperson. And, frequently, he criticizes any mistakes the salesperson is foolish enough to admit.

The salesperson will describe you and answer questions in a way designed to guide the manager into doing whatever the salesperson thinks is best. This is why you should tell the salesperson you're sold on the car, you're sold on the store, and you want to do the deal right now:

- The closer she feels to her commission, the harder she'll try to persuade the manager to accept your deal.
- Your readiness to deal is almost as important to the manager as to the salesperson: money now is both more certain and more valuable than money later. Your readiness to do the deal will increase the manager's willingness to accept the deal you want to do.

So, at least to begin with, use the carrot more than the stick. You will gain more control over salespeople by saying you want to make a deal than by threatening to deal somewhere else. You can always make the threat later. But before that, heighten the salesperson's desire for the deal, just as she heightens your desire for the car. Make her smell the money; make her feel she's only a fraction of an inch away from earning her commission.

Of course, if you are a person who hates to haggle, who cannot feel comfortable with the unscripted theater of bargaining, then simply leave. Assert again the price you are willing to pay, ask for your deposit back, and walk out.

The Manager Doesn't React to the Ball Price

Sometimes, instead of reacting to your price or making a counteroffer, the manager has the salesperson mount an attack on the offer, telling you in ten different ways that it is obviously, ridiculously too low.

Don't waver. Say that you were quoted that price. But maybe she's right. Can she prove it? Then ask to see the invoice: the whole invoice, including the cost figures, not just the retail figures. Don't say this belligerently. You do not want to threaten or antagonize her; you want to give her the means to threaten her manager. The way to do that is to convince her that you're a heck of a nice person, but just about impossible to deal with.

Make that your basic move. Use it whenever your salesperson mounts a powerful defense against your wishes. At the same time, provide her with an excuse with which to protect herself from the manager's anger: some car store managers are bullies and nothing brings out their nasty streak like a request for an invoice.

If you do this unwaveringly and you have an experienced salesperson, you will get the deal you want in fairly short order.

If, however, you have an inexperienced salesperson, or

one the manager doesn't like, or if the manager feels unusually tough and feisty that day, you may get stonewalled.

The Manager Refuses to Counter Your Offer

The manager will not write another offer on the order form and the salesperson will not mention one. In this case, the manager will tell the salesperson that your offer is so low that it makes no sense for him to "commit the house" yet. He will instruct the salesperson to draw a higher offer out of you before he (the manager) offers a lower price.

"Commit the house" means stand by the offer. Normally, a manager's offer equals the house offer equals the deal you get if you accept. And, normally, when the salesperson says that the manager offered such and such, he is quoting, and the offer is for real. If you accept it, you have the deal. But when a salesperson says, "What if I could lease you the car for [x] dollars," and you accept, it means nothing until the manager accepts your acceptance.

If the manager makes no counter, the salesperson will say something like: "Look, we're just not in the right ballpark here. We have to get realistic. A car like this is worth a lot more than you're offering."

Even if you intend to bargain till the night grows old, do nothing. The house should come down before you come up. Come down in concrete terms, not in terms of the salesperson's "If I could, would you." Tell the salesperson you want a counteroffer from the manager. If he answers by talking yet again about wrong ballparks and such, ignore him. Don't waste your energy. Think about the beach again. Be silent.

The enormous pressure of your silence will work quickly. He'll ask what's wrong.

Tell him again that you need a counteroffer. You can't do anything till you get a counteroffer.

He'll say, "Well, what if I could lease you the car for . . ." You say, "No, not what if you could do this or that. An offer from the manager."

Tell him that you really want to do business with him. But, since you know they have some kind of discount in mind to start with, you need to know what it is. You have to know where you're starting from. Otherwise, you're dead in the water.

This gives him an explanation for the manager. It blames the manager; it deflects the burden of incompetence the manager will try to lay on him. Remember, if a manager suspects that you are refusing to pay more because the salesperson is not doing his job properly, he may be unwilling to lower her price.

When the salesperson goes away this time, he'll come back with a counter. If the counteroffer is high, do nothing. Make no offer. Stare at the salesperson as if he were wearing a headdress of toads. He'll ask you what's wrong. He'll tell you the manager just offered you a super discount.

Do the following:

Complain. Tell the salesperson you can't understand what's going on. You thought you could get a good deal here. But the manager didn't take anything off!

They'll tell you it is a good deal. The only reason you don't think so is that your idea of the price is far too low, completely unrealistic.

Ask why is it too low? Is it below cost? Then deliver the punchline: ask to see the invoice, so you can find out for yourself whom to believe. Insist on this issue. What is the cost of the car?

If the salesperson seems too inexperienced to know what

cost is, tell him to find out from the manager. Tell him you have a problem with these wildly differing prices from different dealers and you need to find out what's going on. Were you given a price below cost? What is the cost. . . .

If your salesperson turns a little nasty, if he keeps belittling your offer, or if he tries to act tough, stonewalling you or bullying you, bully him back. Tell him that the high counteroffer is so far over the other dealers' prices that it's insulting. Is he going to explain why it's so high, or just sit there and keep insulting you? And if he's not willing to explain, maybe he should give back your deposit.

Give back money? This is like a brush with death. A close brush with death.

So he'll go see the manager and report what you've said. He'll describe the difficulty he's having with you, emphasizing and exaggerating how close you were to walking out the door. He'll do everything he can to sell the manager the idea that you have to get a good deal. And now you'll either have your deal, or the manager will make a reasonable counteroffer and you'll say good-bye to 50 percent or more of the markup.

After losing half the markup on an inexpensive car like an Escort, you have only a little further to go before you reach a great deal. But on a car marked up a thousand or more, you will still have a way to go.

Haggling

Look disappointed. Complain. Work the deal. Do some horse trading. Make a series of verbal offers, coming up in small increments, always trying to draw lower offers from the salesperson. Use the tried and true "If I could, would you." "What if I could come up with another twenty dollars?

What would that be, fifty cents a month? Could we do business?"

If she says no, come up, maybe, $45 on the price. And say that "forty-five" as if it were forty-five thousand.

After your offer has grown to, say, $50 to $75 more than the first, have it written, sign it, and insist that she take it to the manager.

If necessary, grow somewhat indignant. Tell her you keep offering more and more and she keeps saying no. Well, you're unhappy. She'd better do everything she can to get you this one. No matter how much she protests that you're not being realistic, or you're way off base, or you're playing football with a hockey puck, or whatever. You have been offering more and more. What does she want, blood? She'd better give this one a shot for you, her best shot.

She'll go up to the boss and come back with a lower offer.

In this fashion, back and forth—making tiny verbal increases, then writing and signing the offer every time the price goes $30 to $60 beyond the previous one—work your way up.

Don't worry about how many times the salesperson goes back and forth between you and the manager. I've done it seven or eight times and have seen others do it as many as twelve times. You have plenty of time—make sure you have plenty of time—and you have plenty of room. Assuming freight is $300 to $500 and the house pack is $150, you have $450 to $650 worth of room before you get to dealer cost. If you are coming up $50 or $60 each time you make a signed offer, you can make quite a few of them before you arrive anywhere serious. And if you want to get persnickety, ask them to recalculate the lease payment every time you make a higher offer.

Time after time, the salesperson will carry your offer to

the boss—yet still be unable to put the house into profit. At some point, the manager should admit that you know what you want and are determined to have it. Then he'll get off his price and make a serious move toward yours.

The Manager Turns Stubborn and Runs a Bluff

At some point while the house offer is still high, the manager may decide to beat the drums and fire the guns and see if he can scare you into taking his deal.

This will be like the medium counter in the direct approach—only it will be all out. The manager will stand on his previous offer and tell the salesperson to hammer you. Very possibly, he'll bluff the salesperson, too, telling her to get the price or lose the deal.

Then, with you, she will insist, over and over, that they are down to the bone; there is no more markup left to take off; they can go no lower. Nobody can. Nobody can beat the deal they're offering. She will speak with the voice of authority; if she's any good, she will sound like she's telling the truth.

Next, she may employ pressure tactics: tell you that the factory raised the price of the car; try to wear you down; show you spurious documents; downgrade your trade with a vengeance (if you have one); and try to humiliate you by saying maybe you are looking at too much car, maybe you should switch to a less expensive one—or maybe you should think about a used car.

You know what to do.

Point out that what she's saying may be true, but if she wants your business, she will have to prove it. Proof is the invoice, the cost part of the invoice.

Resistance to Showing the Invoice

· The salesperson may ask you what business you're in. Suppose you are in water heaters. She'll ask, "If I bought a water heater from you, would you show me the invoice?"

You say: "No, I wouldn't. But this is the car business." That line will explain almost anything you want it to. It means simply that since cars are the only store-bought item you bargain over, everything is different. As, in fact, it is.

· She may tell you that she really wants to show you the invoice. But she's not allowed to: store policy forbids it.

Say: "But your manager can do it anyway. So tell your manager I need to see it."

· She may say that even the manager isn't allowed to show invoices. The owner won't let him.

Say: "Well, you'd better give the owner a call. Or you'd better give back my deposit."

If you follow the suggestions above, you should get your deal. Be persistent and be consistent — don't waver.

Remind your salesperson that you are the customer and the customer is always right. Don't be bashful about saying that. It will remind her that she has to earn your good will and your business.

But sometimes the folks at the dealership cannot give you the deal you want until they try their knockout punch: the T.O.

The Turnover

After the salesperson fails a number of times to raise you, either a "closer" (a specialist in making deals with difficult customers) or a manager comes in. It's someone new, a fresh face, someone full of energy, ready to work you over, ready to tell you that you can't buy steak for the price of baloney.

Don't be intimidated. And if it's a manager, don't feel flattered to be dealing with a honcho. Simply follow the script laid out above, starting from wherever you are in the deal. Be sure to

(a) say that you thought this store gave good deals and

(b) blame the manager.

Blame the manager for all preceding failures to make the deal. Say that you like the place and you like Rodney or Sally Salespro and you really want to do business with them. But you are not going to do business if the manager won't let the salesperson give you a half-decent deal.

The manager may respond by getting tough. In a stern, no-nonsense voice, he will basically repeat the salesperson's moves. But the message will be: "I know what I'm talking about. I'm the boss."

No matter how bosslike and tough the manager is, even if he's a lot tougher than you, don't waver. Do what you did before: remind him that he needs you more than you need him; make him justify whatever he says; and lead him to cost and the invoice.

A Little secret about T.O.'s: Once a manager hoists his butt off his seat, rarely will he let you go without making a deal. He'll spend a decade or two trying to force the salesperson to get an $800 or a $1,000 profit. The salesperson fails and fails. The manager makes her feel like a total incompetent, a walking failure factory.

Then the manager takes control. This is a big-time honcho you're dealing with here. He knows the car business inside and out. He knows every move ever made. You don't have a chance; there's no way you're going to beat this guy in a deal. And then he closes you.

At $250 over cost.

A Deal with a Trade

When you trade in, the deal is a little more complicated. Assuming that you use your trade equity as a down payment, there will be a couple more numbers for you to consider — and therefore a couple more ways for you to be hoodwinked.

If you put the trade equity down on the lease, then sell price minus trade allowance equals cash difference. If you owe nothing on the trade and put nothing else down, then the cash difference will equal the capitalized cost, or acquisition cost, for the leased car.

If, however, you owe money on the trade, you must add back the lien payoff. Then the acquisition cost equals the cash difference plus the amount needed to pay off the lien.

What You Will Be Paid for Your Trade

You will be paid wholesale or less: the least you'll take. The most you can get is wholesale plus the maximum discount you can negotiate on the new car.

However, you will also effectively receive whatever the sales tax would be on that amount of money. In many states, you pay no sales tax on a down payment made with trade equity. Why? Because you've already paid sales tax on that money. On the other hand, in most states, cash down is taxed at the standard rate. Put down $2,000 cash in a state that charges 6% and you'll pay $120 in tax on it. In effect, then, a trade worth $2,000 will bring you $2,120.

A *Little Inside Info*

Wholesale, or cash value, is called "hard money" or "hard dollars" or simply "hard," as in "two thousand hard." Your discount is known as "show money" or "show dollars."

Most salespeople know these words. But not many know the actual numbers involved. Which doesn't matter anyway, for your salesperson has no say in deciding what your car is worth. Managers have the say; managers make the decision.

Managers also run the salespeople during deals. They tell them what to say, how much to ask for the store's car, how much to offer for your car, when to offer you more, and so on. They continually ask the salesperson what you are doing and saying and thinking: trying to figure you out from afar. They question and control the salesperson with varying degrees of strictness, depending on their opinion of his or her ability. But they control the deal absolutely, deciding how much you will pay for the new car and how much they will pay for your car.

This is an extremely important part of their job. A manager's mandate is to limit as far as possible the amount of money the store invests in trade-ins. Too much money tied up in used cars will kill a dealership. This is because almost every deal with a trade represents negative cash flow until the trade is sold.

The Wash Sheet

However, when a deal first appears in the store's bookkeeping, the cash flow is shown as positive. Here's how a manager figures out (washes) a deal with a trade, whether a lease or a buy.

Selling price   _____
minus Trade allowance   − _____
equals Cash difference   = _____
plus Wholesale value of trade   + _____
equals Gross   = _____
minus Cost of unit (including pack)   − _____
equals Net before commission   = _____

The form with these blanks, called a "wash sheet," is written out for every deal. Every trade taken in is pegged with a wholesale value. So the manager's evaluation of your car appears instantly — and stays there forever — for everyone to see. You can imagine how much the manager wants his estimate to be right.

Although the wholesale value of the trade is entered on the wash sheet as a positive number, that money does not, in fact, exist until your car is sold. And if the salesperson's commission is paid before someone buys your car, it too represents negative cash flow: money paid out before it comes in.

To illustrate, suppose you were trading in a car worth $4,000 hard on a new car retailing for $15,000 and marked up $1,500 after the pack. You come in wanting $5,500 for your car.

Obviously, you won't get it, for that would be $1,500 over its cash value. That is to say, it would be a discount of $1,500 on a car that was marked up $1,500: an even swap with a bottom line of zero.

After a long negotiation, you finally accept $4,700. That's your trade allowance — "show dollars." The salesman "shows you" $4,700. Here's how the manager would wash the deal:

Selling price	$15,000
Trade allowance	−$4,700
Cash difference	=$10,300
Wholesale value of trade	+$4,000
Gross	=$14,300
Cost of unit	−$13,500
Net before commission	=$800

The "net before commission" you see here is also called the gross profit, or, simply, the gross. This one is medium-sized. Big grosses are, of course, everybody's dream but yours. Notice that, although a profit is shown, what you are actually leasing the car for is $10,300, the cash difference.

When the dealership drafts on the lease contract (requests and receives payment) that's what the lessor will pay. The dealer, however, will have to pay the factory or the bank that financed the car approximately $13,000: the $13,500 cost of unit minus the pack and the holdback. Therefore, the store will be in the red for about $2,700 ($13,000 paid out, $10,300 taken in). And if the salesperson receives a commission of $160 or so before your car is sold, the store will be in the red for $2,860.

The Meaning of "Actual"

I'm going through this so you understand what "wholesale value" and "actual cash value" really mean and how great the pressure is not to exceed them. These phrases refer to the amount of money your car can be sold for immediately, the very next day, if necessary, to turn the deal into positive cash flow: sold either at the auction or to the used car dealer down the block. Very few stores can afford to have a bunch of money-losing deals sitting around without knowing precisely when they can be turned into money-making deals.

But, you may ask, since wholesale value is an estimate, how can it be considered "hard" money? Because the selling prices of used cars are monitored daily and the results published every week. That's why I emphasize finding the right used car price guide (see page 84). The books wholesalers use report the amounts various cars brought at auction sales no longer ago than the previous week. Subtract a few dollars and that's what your car will bring this week.

What Does This Mean to You?

No matter where you do the deal, no matter how you try to negotiate—whether you start by hiding the fact that you have a trade, or start by emphasizing what you want for the trade, or start with everything at once—you will not be paid more than actual cash value. But if you don't find out what that is ahead of time, you may be paid less and still receive what seems to be a magnificent sum as a trade allowance.

If you want to know the price you're paying to lease your new car, you must know the cash value of your trade. You can't work from discount or trade allowance. The price of a new car equals the cash difference plus the cash value of the trade-in. Add the two and that's the price. Subtract the cost of the unit with pack and that's the dealer's gross profit.

Doing It with a Trade

Let's suppose you have looked up the value of your old car in the current wholesale price book that your local dealers use. You've followed directions carefully and determined that wholesale on the car is $2,000.

The new car will be a four-wheel-drive sport utility, like

a Blazer, Explorer, or Pathfinder, and now's a good time to get one. The current popularity of these vehicles has pushed their residual values to nearly absurd heights.

Let's say you like the Blazer, moderately well equipped, at a sticker price of $26,000, including $500 for freight. There may be a package discount or a rebate of around $500, but we'll ignore them here in favor of simplicity.

The residual values we will use are 63%, 59%, 51%, and 45% for lease terms of 24, 36, 48, and 60 months respectively. We'll use a lease rate of 8.5 percent and a money factor of .00354.

Assume that a cost/price book shows invoice cost to be $23,100. Freight brings it to $23,600. Finance and advertising costs raise it to $23,900. (Numbers rounded off.)

Now, adding $100 for the pack gives a dealer cost of $24,000.

Thus we have four costs:

Cost without freight:	$23,100
Cost with freight:	$23,600
Invoice cost (with finance and ad):	$23,900
Dealer cost (with [low] pack):	$24,000

After $24,000 we are into profit for the house. We add amounts to dealer cost to give us a price based on a specific profit.

For example:

Dealer cost:	$24,000
+ $200 for profit:	$24,200
+ $300 for profit:	$24,300
+ $400 for profit:	$24,400
+ $500 for profit:	$24,500

+ $600 for profit: $24,600
+ $1,000 for profit: $25,000

And so on up to sticker price: $26,000.

Let's say you're willing to pay up to $600 over dealer cost. That particular deal would look like this:

Dealer Cost + Profit = Price   − Wholesale for Trade = Cash Difference
   $24,000 + $600 = $24,600 − $2,000   = 22,600

In this case, since you're not putting any cash down or buying any add-ons, and we are (optimistically) assuming no bank fees, $22,600 would be the capitalized cost on the lease.

As you can see, selling price minus the wholesale value or cash value of your trade equals the cash difference. Reversing the operation shows that the price you pay for the new car is the cash difference plus the wholesale value of your trade.

How Far and How Long?

Now you have to decide how many miles you'll probably drive and how long you'll want the truck.

If there are factory subsidized leases, they will be for 24 to 36 months. But the mileage allowances and penalties for excess mileage may vary widely. When you're checking the papers for bargains read the small print carefully. There's no point chasing a hot deal if you drive 14,000 miles a year and the bargain lease allows only 10,000.

Lease Terms and Payments Compared

Under the terms laid out above ($600 over, $2,000 for your trade, capitalized cost of $22,600, residual factors of .63, .59, .51, .45, and a base lease rate of 8.5%), we get the following payments:

24-MONTH PAYMENT
(8.5% rate): $397.17
(7.5% rate): $380.98
(7% rate): $372.86
(4% rate): $324.14

36-MONTH PAYMENT
(8.5% rate): $335.97
(7.5% rate): $320.23
(7% rate): $312.33
(4% rate): $264.88

48-MONTH PAYMENT
(8.5% rate): $321.52
(7.5% rate): $306.64

60-MONTH PAYMENT
(8.5% rate): $303.09

The lower rates indicate one method of factory subsidization. There won't be any on 60-month deals, and, probably, no 48-month deals. You can see from the payments above that in terms of quality, or at least "newness," received for money spent, the 36-month lease is probably the best deal. And you can probably see why: the fourth and fifth years represent large drops in residual value. Note that this is not the same for each make and model. Vehicles shed value at different rates and at different times.

Unless the decision as to the length of term is determined by the payment, keep in mind (a) the length of the warranty and (b) the amount of time you want to elapse between the fuss and bother of getting a new car.

Are there any reasons to consider longer lease terms? Not in the pure numbers. But in your expectations for future earnings and expenditures, there may be. I ran these numbers a little over two years ago, on a Blazer with a tad more equipment. This year's (1998) numbers are over 10 percent higher. Lease payments rose at a pace more than twice as great as the rate of inflation, due to the cost of the vehicle. If you think your income will be flat for four or five years and then rise, or if you plan to incur a major financial burden in two years (e.g., have children, buy a house), you might not want a short-term lease. You might want the longest lease you can get in order to keep the payments stable for the longest period of time. Consider length of term not just in light of the residual values for the particular vehicle, but also in light of your own earning and family circumstances.

But whatever the term, the folks at the car store will not want to discuss your lease the way we have here.

Store Policy: Work from Sticker Price Down — Not from Cost Up

Your salesperson and the manager will try to deal from retail or sticker price. If the deal is settled at a cash difference of $22,600, they will try to show you something like this (discounting the truck's price a bit for appearance' sake):

Price − Trade Allowance = Cash Difference
$25,600 − $3,000   = $22,600

Remember, a trade allowance is the cash value of the trade-in (hard dollars) plus the amount discounted off the agreed-upon price of the new car (show dollars).

No one will want to discuss these distinctions with you because managers and salespeople have learned that working from high prices and showing discounts as big trade allowances is more effective, both in satisfying customers and in getting big grosses. Notice that "both." People will sometimes pay more so they can believe they got more for their old car.

To determine the cash difference, then, the store will not subtract wholesale from a discounted price; it will subtract trade allowance (wholesale plus discount) from a retail price that has been discounted only slightly to show the store gives good deals.

Working from Cost Up to Establish Cash Difference

In the example, our trade equity is serving as a down payment. We are putting no other money down and we owe nothing on the trade. Therefore, the cash difference will equal the lease acquisition cost or capitalized cost.

Now, if you were going out to lease the Blazer, all you would really have to do is set the numbers at the highest amount you are willing to pay, or $600 over dealer cost.

But that is not what you *should* do. The more familiar you are with the entire range of possible numbers on the vehicles in question, the less likely you are to be victimized.

You should prepare something like this: a list of costs, profits, sell prices, cash differences (price minus wholesale value), lease payments based on those cash differences, and trade allowances. The list should range from the lowest offer you are likely to make to the highest price they are likely to ask. Something like the list below, based on a 36-month term, a 59% residual value, and an 8.5% rate (.00354 money factor).

	Cost/ Sell Price	Wsle. on Trade	Cash Diff.	Trade Allow.	Lease Payt.
$1,000 under invoice cost:	$22,900	−$2,000=	$20,900	$5,100	$282.73
Cost less freight:	$23,400	−$2,000=	$21,400	$4,600	$298.39
Dead (invoice) cost:	$23,900	−$2,000=	$21,900	$4,100	$314.05
Cost + $100 pack or Dealer Cost:	$24,000	−$2,000=	$22,000	$4,000	$317.18

When we add profit, cost becomes . . . price.

Dlr. Cost + $100:	$24,100	−$2,000= $22,100	$3,900	$320.31
Plus $200:	$24,200	−$2,000= $22,200	$3,800	$323.45
Plus $300:	$24,300	−$2,000= $22,300	$3,700	$326.58
Plus $400:	$24,400	−$2,000= $22,400	$3,600	$329.72
Plus $500:	$24,500	−$2,000= $22,500	$3,500	$332.85
Plus $600:	$24,600	−$2,000= $22,600	$3,400	$335.97
Plus $700:	$24,700	−$2,000= $22,700	$3,300	$339.12
Plus $800:	$24,800	−$2,000= $22,800	$3,200	$342.26
Plus $1,000:	$25,000	−$2,000= $23,000	$3,000	$348.53
Plus $1,800:	$25,800	−$2,000 $23,800	$2,200	$373.53
At sticker:	$26,000	−$2,000= $24,000	$2,000	$379.80
At sticker:	$25,000	−$1,000= $24,000	$1,000	$379.80
Sticker + $500:	$26,000	−$1,500= $24,500	$1,500	$395.47

Note: Payment is rising about $3.132 per $100 of capitalized cost. So if there were a bank fee of, say, $300 factored into the payments, each payment would be about $9.40 higher.

Notice in the last items that the selling price doesn't matter. What matters is the cash difference, or capitalized cost. Therefore, if your car is worth $2,000 actual cash and you are convinced to accept $1,000 for it, you pay sticker even though you have received a $1,000 discount off the selling price. And, if you are charged $26,000, or sticker price but receive $500 less than the cash value of your trade, you are in reality paying $500 over sticker. This may not be easy for them to do if your trade-in were worth $2,000, but it would be easier with a trade worth, say, $8,750.

How, you ask, could you get sucked into that last payment at $500 over sticker? Suppose you came in and they told you it would cost you $610 a month, before taxes, to buy the truck on a four-year loan. Then the guy says you can lease it for three years for $425. Then he says, wait a minute. He goes off to talk to the boss and comes back and says, no, no, I was wrong. Not $425, only $395.47. Just pay the taxes up front. Sign right here.

Now, that would never work on you—but it has worked on other people. Remember that price equals cash difference plus wholesale value of trade.

If making a list like this seems to be a lot of work, bear in mind that the more familiar you are with the entire range of numbers, the better you will understand every aspect of your deal and every offer your salesperson makes. A fringe benefit is that it enables you to see the difference that adding or subtracting $100 from the price makes in the lease payment. To make your own list, just use the format above and plug in your own numbers.

If You Hate Numbers

If you have a mental block against numbers, can only handle one or two at a time, and therefore must think in terms of sticker price minus trade allowance, do this:

Figure out the effective (after pack) markup on the car: Sticker price of $26,000 minus dealer cost (including pack) of $24,000 equals an effective markup of $2,000.

From that, subtract the amount of profit you are willing to pay: $2,000 − $600 = $1,400. That is, $1,400 is the size of the (smallest) discount you will accept.

Now add the discount of $1,400 to the cash value of your car: $1,400 + $2,000 = $3,400 trade allowance. You will buy the truck at sticker with $3,400 being the least you'll take for your car.

Subtract that trade allowance from the sticker price ($26,000 − $3,400 = $22,600) and you have a cash difference—which will be the lease's capitalized cost—of $22,600.

Why is the first method better, if they amount to the same thing?

Too many people worry about what they are getting "off." But the size of the discount is irrelevant. After all, dealers add protection packages and decor groups so they can show big discounts while sacrificing very little profit. Profit is what counts: the amount over cost. Make the effort to list all the costs, profits, cash differences, and so on. Worry about the amount the dealer is putting on, not the amount you are getting off.

At the Dealership

A deal with a trade is the same as one without—except there's one more item and a few more numbers with which the salesperson can try to confuse you. Here are the basic moves you'll encounter. (Remember, if you determine the cash value of your car and the dealer cost of the new car, you will not be easily confused.) Here are a few of the basic tactics.

1. They will start with a low offer for your car. The salesperson will avoid telling you what he thinks your car is worth. He'll try to find out what you want for it, and how much you can spend per month, then tell the manager. Normally, the manager will tell him to start with a low offer for your car. If your car was worth $12,000 the offer would be around $10,500. With our hypothetical car worth $2,000, the first offer would be around $1,000.

Having run the range of numbers, you would spot this immediately. And come back with the $282 payment that begins the list. That's why you should start your list so low: it gives you an offer that should rattle the salesperson's chain, informing him that if he tries to jerk you around, you will jerk back.

2. They will knock your socks off with an astounding offer for your car. If your car's worth two and you ask for three, they'll offer you $4,500. The point is to make you go, "Hot damn, I got it, this baby is mine!" In other words, to make you commit emotionally to having the Blazer. Then, as mentioned, they whittle away at the value of your trade. In theory, you know your car's not worth that much money, so you'll accept successively lower offers without letting go of the Blazer.

Since you've discovered and accepted as reality the cash value of your car, you simply sign that high offer and hand over a deposit. Then assume the high moral ground and watch your salesperson squirm as they try to knock $2,000 off the original offer.

If they do neither of these things, you would simply do as we discussed earlier. Either take the direct approach and state the deal you want, repeating it till you get it. Or, begin negotiation by stating you have been offered the vehicle at cost less freight less the wholesale value of your car: the ball price.

As soon as you state a figure, the salesperson will ask where in the world you got your numbers. Answer: From other salespeople. Ask him: Why is his price, payment, or trade allowance so much higher (or lower) than other dealers? *Ask him to justify his numbers rather than bothering to justify yours.*

Whatever his numbers are, whether he has started with a low offer for your car, or he has told you he could get you more than twice what it is worth, let's assume the lease payment he is quoting you is the same, around $364 a month. He'll write that payment on the purchase order form (or, if he's clever, drop the payment by $9 or $10) and push it over to you, asking you to okay it—i.e., sign it.

If you've done your homework, you know from the list of numbers you crunched that this payment represents a profit of $1,400 to $1,600. The way you start forcing him to justify this price/payment is to force him to write every step in the payment calculation on the purchase order form. The mere act of putting all the terms in writing will constitute an attack on the salesperson's price—and he will know it. For, as I've mentioned, all that will appear on the form will be something like this: "Customer will lease for 36 months at $364.19 a month, plus tax and trade." However, with all the terms spelled out, it would look something like this:

Retail price	$26,000.00
Trade allowance	−$2,500.00
Cash difference/Capitalized cost	$23,500.00
36-month lease payment based on capitalized cost of $23,500	$364.19
	plus tax

Or like this:

Selling price	$25,500.00
Wholesale value of trade	−$2,000.00
Cash difference/Capitalized cost	$23,500.00
Lease payment	$364.19
	plus tax

They don't want you to know that their price is so high, and their offer for your trade is so low, so you can see why it won't say this. Demand that it does. *If necessary, you write it*: "Retail price: $26,000. Then write "trade" and ask what you are being paid for your car.

The salesperson may pull a figure out of the air, something he thinks you'll accept, and say: "Oh, around forty-five hundred." Or he may head for the manager's desk to find out what to say. Assume that he says $4,500. Whatever it is, write it on the purchase order.

Retail price	$26,000
Trade allowance	−$4,500
Cash difference	$21,500

Then write, "36-month lease payment based on $21,500."

Then say, "You figured your $364 lease payment on a cap cost of twenty-one-five?"

Then shut up and stare at him.

If he didn't realize he had a problem before, he'll realize it now. He'll look at you as if The Alien were popping out of your skull.

When he recovers, he'll try to evade your questions. Be patient for a little while; he has to do this, it's his job. But after that little while goes by, point out to him that he should answer questions you are completely entitled to ask.

Now he's stuck. He will probably go see the manager to find out what to tell you. When he comes back, he may admit making a mistake or he may try to be stern and to bully you, as before, telling you that you know very well that your car's not worth $4,500, so, if you are serious, you'd better get realistic. And then, of course, he'll do his absolute best to get you any kind of realistic or reasonable figure.

Now go with whatever you have chosen: the direct approach or the negotiation. And things will be pretty much as before — except there are more items to have written down on the purchase order.

These extra items may create an extra problem with the manager. He may ignore your requests and persist in countering your offers with: "Dear Ms. or Mr. Jones, we need

$355.50 (or whatever) a month for 36 months plus tax and trade."

Tell the salesperson to inform the manager that you *have* to have everything written on the purchase order form. Dangle the carrot; show the stick. Tell him the place has a good reputation and you really want to do business there — but if they refuse to write everything down, you'll have to go somewhere else.

And be willing to do it; be willing to actually walk out.

Once they've started writing down the basic information discussed above, start pressing them to write down each step in the calculation of the lease payment.

Typical Dodges

1. The salesperson may tell you not to worry about having things written down. Just wait till the business manager puts it on the computer, then you'll see everything on the Regulation M truth in leasing form. That's the government form, he'll tell you. Everything will be there, by law.

Refuse. You want it now, on the purchase order form. Or, since they have brought up Regulation M, you want it on that form. Now.

2. He may say they can't do it now, because they don't have the information till the computer figures it out. This is nonsense. Anyone with a pencil and a five dollar calculator can figure out a lease payment. Threaten to leave.

And be willing to do it. You are the customer; you are correct to request this information in writing and you are entitled to it. So go after it. Accept no excuses, and you'll get it. And once they start writing things down, you have gone a long way down the road toward a good deal.

AVOIDING AFTERSHOCK:
What Happens If You Want to End the Lease Early or Buy the Car at the End of the Lease

There are snares and pitfalls in everything, right? In leasing, the major snare, the big bugaboo, is the problem of early termination, whether voluntary or forced.

Buying the car at the end of the lease is but a minor snare, a mid-sized bugaboo — but one that has, nonetheless, captured many an innocent consumer and gobbled up an extra five hundred to one thousand of their hard-earned dollars.

Why would you want to end a lease early? Circumstances change. You may have a car that no longer suits you — or you can no longer afford. Or that you hate. Or that your new spouse hates.

And why buy a car at the end of the lease? It may be the best you've ever had. Or you may want to give it to a family member. Or you may be suffering from sticker shock and not want to spend the money for a new car. Whatever, as the saying goes.

In this chapter, I'll show you how to minimize the risk, and potential cost, involved in these difficult situations.

EARLY BUYOUTS AND FORCED TERMINATIONS

Ending a lease early is a problem simply because you must, of course, pay off the lease. During the first few months, however, your car will drop in value by the amount of all the dealer charges, including profit, finance and advertising charges, freight, and so on, over its cost—plus its depreciation for time and wear. In a few short months your car may depreciate 20 to 30 percent. Clearly, your payments will not cover this loss in value. And, as the months go by, the amount you have to pay to make up the difference will not necessarily go down.

Whether you buy or lease, the car may continue to depreciate faster than you are paying it off. If you want to end either an installment purchase loan or a lease early, the sum you are obligated to pay can be painfully large. The lower lease payment, which means a slower payoff, can make that sum even larger and more painful. On top of that, the typical lessor's attempt to impose penalties and to recover more interest faster can further aggravate the situation.

YOUR LEASE AGREEMENT

Help from Regulation M?

The new consumer protection law does not do as much for you here as might be hoped. As you may recall, it requires a statement of the conditions under which the lease may be terminated early, and a statement of any penalty or other charges, "which must be reasonable." And it requires a warning that these charges may be "up to several thousand dollars."

That looks to me as if there's an awful lot of latitude in the definition of "reasonable." So let's take a look at what you want and what various contracts may offer you.

What You Want and What You May Get

What you want is a closed-end lease that includes a purchase option at no charge. You also want — but may not be able to have — the purchase option, with no pre-payment penalty, to be in effect throughout the lease term.

Why is this important? Changing circumstances. For example, I know two families who have leased pickup trucks. At the moment I write this, both trucks have been sitting unused for months. These trucks will continue to sit; the people will continue to pay.

There are two ways out of this situation, two forms of voluntary early termination. One is to return the vehicle and pay the balance owed, as defined in your lease contract. The other, often less expensive, is to sell the vehicle and use the proceeds to pay or help pay the balance owed.

But you cannot sell the car unless the contract permits you to buy it. And that balance owed on the lease may be defined in several different ways, some of them not at all friendly to your economic interests.

Typical Early Termination and Early Buyout Provisions

Some of these may change by the time you read this, but most will not. You will probably encounter, or may already have, a lease contract containing some combination of them.

Many bank leases flatly forbid early buyouts. Banks want

to collect all the interest. A bank in Pennsylvania not only prohibits early buyouts, but, if you must terminate the lease early, places you in default and requires you to return the car and pay all of the remaining lease payments, including interest.

Another lender's contract gives you no right to early termination—unless it is agreed to in writing by you, the dealer, and the lessor.

If everybody does agree in writing, the contract states that to pay off the lease you will have to pay: all of the remaining monthly payments with no rebate for unearned interest, plus the residual value, minus the amount the lessor receives when it sells the car. This looks like a real deal killer. However, it, too, can be changed—if agreed to in writing by you, the dealer, and the lessor.

The requirements of other lessors range from this extreme—no buyout, return the car, make all the payments, pay a penalty—to the other, which is most favorable to you: buyout or lease payoff permitted for the balance of the purchase price with no penalties.

If you buy out the lease, either you keep the car or recover your money by selling it. If you turn it in, the amount you owe is reduced by the amount the lessor realizes when it sells the car.

The kickers, present in most leases, are:

1. An early termination fee or penalty. In my experience, many lessors can be persuaded to forgo these extra charges. It helps if you have leased through a dealer and have persuaded the dealer to go to bat for you.

2. The fact that you pay off depreciation more slowly than you think. You pay off any loan more slowly than you think, but more so on leases. The way earned interest is calculated differs from most consumer installment purchase

loans. With the method used on most leases, more interest is earned faster. When more of your money goes to pay interest, less goes to pay principal, or in this case, depreciation. More principal, or more depreciation, thus remains for you to pay. And don't be fooled by the way your lease payment is expressed when the payment is calculated. You'll see something like this: "$195 Depreciation, $75 Interest [or Lease Charge]."

The money factor that produces this expression of the lease payment is a "constant"; it has nothing to do with the way money is allocated to interest during the course of your payments.

So, unless you're an accountant, don't bother discussing the amortization of the lease balance. Instead, simply discuss the possibility of your buying the car during the term, and the amount you will have to pay for it.

What to Negotiate For

When you're sitting there doing the deal, you can't negotiate for specific numbers, because you don't know what the wholesale value of your car will be, you don't know exactly how your lessor calculates interest earned, and you don't know when you may want to end the lease.

What to do? Get your lessor's contract ahead of time and read it. If it contains items that may hang you in the future, like heavy penalties for early termination, have your salesperson or a manager explain those items until you understand them. Then try to negotiate them out of the contract.

In their place, try to insert a clause stating that you can pay off the lease and buy the car during the term (a) for the balance of the purchase price (or the capitalized cost, if the salesperson argues with the word "price") and (b) without any prepayment penalties. You may be successful.

What to Negotiate for If the Crunch Comes

Let's say you are already driving a leased car when an emergency arises. You have to get out of the car. Sell it, turn it in, whatever. How do you decide what would be the fair price, or calculate the payoff on the loan?

First, make an assumption that is incorrect, but that benefits you. Assume that your lease is a "regular" installment loan, with interest paid on the declining balance. Assume that the amount of the loan is the same as the amount of the lease capitalized cost: i.e., what the lessor paid to acquire the car. Then figure out what it would cost to pay off a loan in the amount of the capitalized cost after x number of months, with x being the number of months that have gone by in your lease.

For the interest rate, use the rate of your lease.

For the term (number of months) of the loan: Use the total number of months for which you originally leased the car.

For the number of months after which you want the remaining balance, use the number that have gone by on your lease.

For example, you leased the car for 48 months. After 24 months, you want out. You need the remaining balance on a 48-month loan after 24 months.

To get the balance, you can use a financial calculator, if you have one. Or you can look it up in a loan amortization chart, in the back of a loan payment book. Or you can call a bank.

If you call the bank, tell them the amount of the loan, the percentage rate, the length of the loan — the same length as your lease—and ask what the payment would be. After you get the payment, ask for the balance remaining after the number of months that have gone by in your lease. They'll give you the answers.

Once you have got the remaining balance of the loan, you have to add in what you would have paid on the loan but did not pay on the lease because of its lower payments. To figure out the amount:

The bank told you the loan payment. Subtract the before-tax lease payment from the loan payment. Then multiply the difference by the number of months your lease has run. The result will be the amount you would have paid on the loan, but haven't paid on the lease. Add it to the balance owed quoted by the bank. The result will be about what it would cost to pay off a loan in the amount of the capitalized cost for your car. In other words: what the lessor would have made on the money it paid for the car if it had lent that money to you instead. That's the amount to shoot for as fair if you want to buy out your lease.

What If You Want to Turn the Car In?

If you want to turn the car in, use the same amount minus the agreed-on wholesale value of the car, or minus the amount that the lessor realizes when it sells the car at whole-sale, whichever the lease contract stipulates.

Remember, your goal is to save money by starting a ne-gotiation. Do *not* start negotiating until you find out the balance due on the lease. It is possible, although quite un-likely, that the balance due on the lease will be lower than that due on the hypothetical purchase loan.

Here's an example: You have leased a vehicle for 48 months with a capitalized cost of $20,000, a residual of $8,300, a lease rate of 9%, and a payment of $349.12. After

24 months you want to buy the vehicle — or need to get rid of it.

When you did the deal, 9% was the going rate on new car loans. The capitalized cost, $20,000, at 9% for 48 months costs $497.80 per month. After two years, you would have paid 24 × $497.80, or $11,947.20. The remaining balance on the loan would be $10,895. Add these two figures: the total is $22,842. This is what it would cost you to borrow the money for four years, then pay off the loan after 24 months.

After 24 months on the lease, you have paid 24 × $349.12, or $8,378.88. Now subtract what you actually paid from what would have been the loan payoff: $22,842 (the total to pay off the loan) minus $8,378 (what you have paid on the lease) equals $14,640. This would be a reasonable price at which to buy out the lease.

If you wanted to buy the car, the lease contract could require you to pay: a $200 early termination fee, plus the remaining depreciation, plus the $8,300 residual value, plus some or all of the interest (or, simply, all of the payments). The total would be between $15,400 and $16,600, depending on how your lessor calculated earned interest. A better deal for you is $14,640.

If you wanted or had to turn in the car, those sums would be reduced by either the car's wholesale value, or what the lessor actually received when selling it. Again, $14,640 is a better deal for you.

Note: One kind of amortization schedule could be run on this lease and yield a balance due after 24 months of $14,400 and change. It is *unlikely* that your lessor will compute its interest earned that way. But anything is possible, so find out what you actually owe before starting to negotiate anything.

What to Say During the Negotiation

When you assert that the balance due on your lease should be lower, you will be told that you're wrong. You will be told that they don't calculate the balance owed the way you have. Don't argue.

Instead, respond by saying that your salesperson told you that, if you had to buy out your lease, the total cost would be about the same as it would be if you bought the car in the first place.

Why? Because many, probably most, salespeople are taught to sell leasing by saying precisely that. So your salesperson may well have said it. Make it a main point, because you are not likely to win an argument about the lessor's accounting principles. Assuming that the cost to pay off the installment loan is less than your lease contract calls for, your points are:

1. The amount is fair.
2. It gives the lessor a decent profit.
3. You were told the buyout would be handled this way; you were told this is about what it would cost.

When negotiating, bear in mind the following:

The car store or lease store wants both good word of mouth and repeat business. They'll probably try to help you. However, they may also try to help themselves by inflating the balance owed so they can make a profit.

Your lessor will almost always be a lender who also makes regular installment purchase loans. The amount you negotiate for may provide less profit than hoped for on a lease. But that profit will nonetheless be one the lender is familiar with. So don't believe your salesperson if she tells you that it simply can't be done because the lessor will not make enough money.

Or don't believe her the first time, anyway. Not all lenders will negotiate these points. But some will, so try. Keep in mind: if you can negotiate a compromise for less than the contract requires, you have won.

WHAT HAPPENS IF THE CAR IS STOLEN OR DESTROYED?

If your car is stolen and never recovered or is totaled in an accident early on in the lease, your insurance company will issue a check for the car's book value. Because cars depreciate most rapidly in the beginning of their lives, that check could fall thousands of dollars short of what you owe on the lease.

Ways Around the Problem

1. A deal with no additional charges

Even if you cannot make a deal for an early voluntary buyout without penalties, shop for, negotiate for—and push hard for—a deal where you pay no penalties and no part of the residual value, nor any other extra costs, if early termination is forced upon you by theft or accidental disaster.

Now, in the wake of Regulation M, such leases are much easier to find than they were only a couple of years ago. Both Ford Credit and Mitsubishi Motor Credit leases, for example, demand only the insurance payment and any deductible subtracted from the insurance payment (plus any unpaid payments due under the lease). That deductible, incidentally, could be as little as $250 or as much as $1,000. It depends on the policy you buy, and some leases permit deductibles as high as $1,000.

Also, in the Philadelphia area, one of the larger lease stores promises that the banks it uses will collect only the balance of their purchase costs should the car be a total loss. If one store can persuade its lenders to do that, so can others.

2. "Gap Insurance."

Gap insurance insures you against the auto insurer's settlement falling short of the balance owed to the lender: it covers the gap. Some lessors automatically include it in your payment. If your lessor does this, check the price, and, because you can pay the premium up front, find out if you are being charged interest on it.

In the Philadelphia area, gap insurance typically costs about 1.5 percent of the monthly lease payment. Check its cost in your area. Don't forget to check with an insurance agent. In my experience, if your lessor includes or offers gap insurance, the price will be good. But that holds true for where I've been and the places I've checked, not necessarily for where you are. So compare the agent's price with the lessor's price.

Gap insurance slightly reduces your savings through leasing—and eliminates the risk of losing thousands, a risk you run whether you lease or buy on time. If you live in a so-called high crime area and/or your vehicle is one that is often stolen, gap insurance probably makes sense.

3. Changing the contract

If your lease contract specifies prepayment penalties in the event of involuntary termination, negotiate to have that clause crossed out, and a new one, charging no prepayment penalties, written in. The salesperson and manager shouldn't give you a hard time about this. All they have to do is call the bank or credit company and ask if the lease will be accepted if it's changed the way you want. If the lessor balks, the manager or the dealership's finance guy can try persuasion. (This sometimes works.) Or he can try to find another lender who will accept the lease the way you want it.

4. Provisions already in the lease: replacement vehicles

Some lease contracts do not require payment of the balance owed. Instead, they require that the lost car be replaced by a substitute. The replacement vehicle can be supplied by either the lessor or the vehicle's insurer. If you refuse to accept the replacement, you are in default on the contract.

Other leases have a similar provision, but could give you a harder time, for some of them make it your responsibility to provide the replacement vehicle. You go out, with insurance money in hand, and buy a used car for the massive financial institution that leased you the car. It's amusing to think of you, or me for that matter, out there waving a puny insurance check and trying to buy a used car for some giant finance company that has access to thousands of used cars at wholesale and billions of dollars in cash, to boot.

And there's still more: other lease contracts give you both options. In case of a total loss, you may (a) pay off the balance owed or (b) "if you and the lessor agree in writing," you may continue the lease with a substitute vehicle.

Check on all of this and make your arrangements when you do the deal. Don't wait until disaster strikes, only to find that your lease is chock-full of user-hostile clauses. And give yourself enough time. Take the contract home and read it. For even though Regulation M requires clear language in leases, certain paragraphs in certain lease contracts will still be written so that most people have a hard time understanding them. If your lease contains any such paragraphs, have them explained thoroughly and, if necessary, changed. And make sure the explanation is precise.

Once you are sure the explanation actually explains what the paragraph means, have either the explanation or the changes you want written into the contract before you sign it. Or even after you sign it—as long as you have not taken delivery of the car. Never forget: no matter how many times a car store manager says, "You bought it, honey or pal," you have not bought the deal and you are not stuck with the car until you drive it off the lot. Until then, you can always demand your deposit back, get it back, and go home.

The involuntary early termination policies you want are:

For replacement cars: That the lessor, lease store, or dealer accepts responsibility to provide, or at least to help you provide, a replacement car. It won't be a new car, by the way. Its age and condition will be similar to yours. You may not like it as much as yours; you make like it more.

For payoffs: Either that you have the option to pay off the balance of the purchase price in lieu of supplying a replacement car, or that the lessor will accept the insurance check (plus the deductible) as full payment for the vehicle.

If your lease says something else, push hard for these changes. You should not be penalized for something over which you have no control.

NEGOTIATING THE END-OF-TERM PURCHASE PRICE

When the lease expires, the end-of-term purchase price (or payoff, or buyout) is the amount you must pay if you want to buy, sell, or trade the car. You must clear your debt to sell or trade the car in, so this amount determines whether or not you have equity in the car: whether you can make any money on it.

In many instances, the lease-end buyout is negotiable. But sometimes it flatly is not. You have to discover for yourself which is the case. The time to try negotiating is right after you reach agreement on price and payment. If you're tired and decide to go home, you may be stuck forever with the high lease-end purchase price written into the contract. Or, if you wait till a couple months before the lease expires and then call the lessor, you are likely to encounter a runaround—or run into a wall of bullpoop. Here's what can happen:

The lessor will tell you that they don't have that information, so you'll have to call your dealer or lease store. The store will tell you they have to check. Then they'll call the lessor—who will get the information from its computer in about a minute. And, finally, the store will call you back and quote a number, a number which will include a four- to five-hundred-dollar markup. We routinely inflated the balance owed on leased vehicles by four to five hundred dollars. Almost every time, for almost every customer. And our practices were very similar to those of many other respectable businesses.

Why does this happen? By forcing you to contact the leasing dealer or lease store, the lessor rewards the place that wrote your lease with an opportunity to do some repeat business. That store now has a chance to lease you another car.

Or, if you buy the car, the store has an opportunity to sell a used car without risking any investment. The dealer handles your buyout as if it were just another sale. You pay off the lien, which is the lessor's buyout, and you pay the dealer's profit. As far as the lessor is concerned, the dealer's profit is his own business.

You cannot get around this cozy little arrangement by calling the lessor and pretending to be Sid Schmelp at Feebleman Motors. For, when you ask for the buyout, the lessor will ask you for your secret code number. They will not tell you the balance owed unless you tell them the secret number. It's like being in a spy movie.

And you can't get around the arrangement by paying your salesperson a few bucks to find out for you. Nine times out of ten your salesperson won't have the code number, either. That number is a closely guarded secret. The dealer changes it periodically and does not tell the salespeople what it is. So the salesperson will have to ask a manager or the finance guy to call the lessor. Whoever makes the call will add the markup before telling the salesperson.

Once, in a fit of research, I called Ford Credit. Telling them I was Joe Paganelli, I asked for my lease buyout. They didn't even bother to find out if a guy named Paganelli had leased a car from them. They said: "We don't have that information. You'll have to call your dealer."

I said I wanted to talk to the manager and, when I got the manager, I immediately began badgering her. I told her I owed the money to Ford and I didn't want to talk to any dealer. I wanted her to tell me what the balance was.

She repeated the same line. I kept on browbeating her, not shouting, but letting my voice rise, and finally she slipped up.

"The amount of the buyout is something you have to negotiate with the dealer," she said. And hung up on me.

Ford Credit is by no means alone in this practice. To do a bit more research, I walked into a randomly chosen bank in Doylestown, Pennsylvania. I said I wanted to speak to someone about my lease buyout.

Very nicely, they said they were very sorry—but I'd have to talk to my dealer.

Obviously, when you talk to your dealer, you cannot negotiate if you don't know that there is a need to negotiate—if you don't even know that there is a negotiable amount involved. And in most cases, no one will tell you.

Many salespeople, in fact, can't tell you. They don't know, either. They believe that the lease buyout or purchase price is like the remaining balance on a loan, which, of course, is not negotiable. They conclude, therefore, that neither is the remaining balance on a lease.

Why Can't You Tell That Something's Fishy?

Because, as I've mentioned, the "official" residual value/buyout/purchase price stated in the lease contract is usually a fairly high retail figure. Often it's so much higher than the actual buyout needed that, even after the dealer adds his four- or five-hundred-dollar profit, the amount quoted to you is lower than you expect.

When this nice, low number comes over the phone, customers are pleasantly surprised. They think they're getting away with something . . . a couple hundred somethings, in fact. So they keep their surprise to themselves and sort of wallow in happiness . . . even as they get burned.

What can you do about this? Negotiate, negotiate, negotiate. And it may not be easy.

If You Have Not Yet Leased the Car

Calculate an estimated buyout. This will be one of your last chores, for to do it you need to know what the terms of the deal will be. Then, determine the going rate on auto loans around town. If it's 9.25%, assume the lender will want at least a 9.25% return on its investment in the leased car.

Then figure out how much the lender actually has at risk, as we did before. Potentially at risk are the sum of your lease payments plus the residual value. Actually at risk is the price of the car: the money paid to buy it, or capitalized cost. (Plus any add-ons, minus any trade equity or cash down.)

Let's go back to the Monte Carlo in chapter 5 for a number and say the lessor has put out $16,500. (In this case, we'll ignore the tax.)

We'll again assume a 48-month lease. Remember, the residual value was $6,237: that will probably be your lease-end purchase price. So, what would $16,500 earn for the lessor over four years at 9.25%?

Get the 4-year 9.25% factor from a loan payment chart: it's .025. Multiply $16,500 by .025. The result is $412.50.

Multiply $412.50 by 48 (months): $19,800. That's the amount collected on $16,500 lent for four years at 9.25%.

Next, get the total of your lease payments. Using the Ford Credit/Monte Carlo numbers for illustration, multiply the before-tax payment of $311.57 by 48 = $14,955.36. Subtract that from the value of the hypothetical loan: $19,800 − $14,955.36 = $4,844.64.

So a buyout of $4,844.64 would provide a 9.25% return on the purchase price of $16,500.

Now you have an idea of what the lessor has to get in order for the investment to make sense at the going rate of interest. It's a great deal lower than the residual of $6,237, isn't it?

Next, if you have a financial calculator, do an amortization schedule for the lease. If you don't have one, call a bank. Tell them you are thinking about leasing and want to find out what the remaining balance would be on a lease with exactly the terms of yours. For this example, my financial calculator tells us that after 48 payments, the remaining balance is $5,184, close to the $5,200 we called the "effective" or wholesale residual value underlying this deal.

Add $100 to $200 for the dealer's or lease store's paperwork and processing: $5,284 to $5,384. Now you have a range. From $4,944 ($4,844 + 100) to about $5,400.

What to Shoot For

You should try for $4,944. Negotiate for a buyout that gives you the car at a total cost no higher than the total cost on a straight installment purchase at the going rate. Plus $100 for the dealer.

Shoot for that, but be willing to settle for a bit more. You should not weep and gnash your teeth if you end up with a buyout of $5,400. Or even $5,500. In our "no free lunch" universe, you cannot reasonably expect to get the benefit of leasing's low payments for free. But you can try.

Possible Exception

You may have searched out the highest possible residual value actually used to figure the payment, resulting in the lowest possible payment. In that case, it will probably be harder to negotiate the buyout, for the lessor will receive a smaller monthly return on its investment.

To illustrate, consider the Monte Carlo put through the bank that was eager for business and used extremely high residuals. The payment, remember, was $291.62.

Now, 48 × $291.62 = $13,997.76.

And $19,800 (earned lending $16,500) − $13,997.76 = $5,802.24

Over the term of the lease, the bank will have collected $1,015 less ($15,012.96 − $13,997.76) on this deal than on the other lease deal we discussed. Therefore, it will probably want to collect some of the interest on that unpaid money. So to your minimum buyout amount of $5,802 you will probably have to add at least a hundred or two in interest plus $100 to $200 in processing fees, making a decent deal on the buyout $6,000 to $6,200.

(However, if you made all your payments then bought the car for the official residual value/lease-end purchase price of $7,256 the bank would collect a total of $13,997.56 + $7,256, or $21,253.76. This is $1,540.56 greater than the amount collected on the loan.)

With a lease deal based on an extremely high residual value, it may be hard to negotiate for a lower buyout. By using the high residual in the first place, however, the bank has indicated that it's hungry for business. So if you wanted the car, it would certainly be worthwhile to try.

Another Possible Exception

The final consideration is the actual cash value of the car. Suppose your official buyout is $7,000, and the amount needed to profit adequately on the loan is $5,500, so you are thinking somewhere around $6,000. But now also suppose that cars like yours are going at wholesale for $6,500.

This means that the day you turn the car in, the lessor can call a local wholesaler and get $6,500 for the car. In this case, they will not sell it to you for $5,700 or $6,000. You'll probably have to pay $6,900 to $7,000. In used car transactions, actual cash value is the controlling factor in the deal.

Negotiating the Buyout Details

Prepare the buyout figures while you are calculating payments, before going in to lease the car. Then, during the deal, you can both test the waters to estimate your chances for success and simultaneously set up the coming negotiation. Ask the salesperson:

What if you want to buy the car at the end of the lease? How will the cost compare to the cost of buying it in the first place? Some stores, and some lenders, will tell you that leasing is designed to give you a low monthly payment, not to finance a buy. This will hint that the buyout will be hard to negotiate.

Others, however, will tell you that the total cost of leasing and buying at the end will be about the same as buying from the beginning. Or within a hundred dollars or so. And they may throw in, "And maybe even less."

Don't do anything more until you've reached an agreement on price. Then, just before signing the final time, say, "Wait a minute. What will the buyout be?"

The salesperson will tell you it will be the amount of the residual value and that you'll see it in the contract.

Tell her, no, you think it should be around $_____: the number you have figured out in advance.

When she asks where you got your figures, explain that buying the car for x dollars at x percent for however long would be so much a month. Multiplied by the number months, that would come to $_____: whatever the total, as we did on page 130. On your lease, however, your payment is x dollars a month times the number of months for a total of $_____.

Subtract this total from the total of the buy payments. Show the salesperson the difference. And say that's what your purchase option price should be.

When she makes noises, ask her: Didn't she just say it would cost about the same to buy at the end of the lease as it would to buy in the first place? And isn't that what you've just showed her?

In Comes the Manager

Your salesperson will probably not know what to do next, so she will go get a manager. Repeat what you just said. If the manager asks for an explanation of your figures, give him the same one.

He will say: "Wrong."

Ask him to explain why.

He may not explain anything. Instead, he may say a couple of things that you should not settle for:

"Don't worry about it, you'll see it in the contract." Or: "We can't give it to you now; it has to be worked out on the computer. So just sign the deal and then we'll take you in to see the business manager and he'll explain everything."

Refuse these invitations. All it takes to figure it out is a pencil, paper, a five dollar calculator, and a couple of minutes. Tell the manager that it has to be taken care of right now. You might mention that you've shopped at a dealer nearby who was willing to cut down the buyout.

But do not be in a hurry to walk out. This is not like going down the street to Fred's Ford and beating a deal by forty dollars. So make your threats mildly, here. But keep in mind that they want to move that unit and they want to move it now, to you. Which provides you with a big stick.

An Argument That May Give You Trouble

The manager may tell you that your low lease payment will not pay off all of the money the lessor pays for the car. Therefore, you'll owe interest on all that unreduced principal.

Don't argue back unless you are an accountant. Instead,

try to brush the whole point aside. Say, "Yeah, but I'll pay [or I have paid, if you're at the end of the lease] as much interest on the lease as I would on the buy—or even more! So it doesn't matter."

This is true, but don't press the point unless you're a numbers whiz. Change the subject.

There's a very good chance that the manager won't bring up this argument. He may, however, bring up an elaborate and specious argument—which could be based on anything at all—"proving" that you are wrong, that your buyout really does equal the residual value. Remember, I "proved" to a customer that I'd given him a $2,000 discount when the actual price was $500 over sticker.

Again, avoid discussion. To answer either of these arguments, tell the manager that however it works, the buyout can't be the same as the residual value. If he asks you to explain, say "Because Sally Salespro here told me that buying the car at the end of the lease would cost the same as it would cost if I bought it on time."

This puts considerable pressure on the manager to justify his figure. To do that, he will have to tell you (a) that interest is accumulating faster than you think (or being paid on a nondeclining balance), making the actual APR higher than the nominal rate, or (b) that the buyout is set higher than it need be, preparing you to pay a profit that you don't know about. He does not want to say those words, not even in his sleep.

End Game

Begin to close the deal with a compromise, to help them save face. How? By repeating yourself, of course.

Say something like this: "Look, Sally said buying the car at the end would cost about the same as what it would cost to buy it in the first place. So the $_____(the residual value) is x dollars too high. So if you take off the x dollars, I could see that. Maybe even fifty dollars more, for the paperwork."

Why offer more before they offer less? To get things rolling: to help the manager see a way to resolve the situation. You may be presenting these folks with something new. And when faced with something new, people sometimes freeze. Motion stops. Progress stops.

And progress could be possible. For the manager's knowledge provides you with a lever. The manager knows, even though the salesperson may not, that the high lease-end purchase price includes a future profit for the store.

However, he has a profit right now. And if you don't buy the car when the lease expires, the amount of the lease payoff is completely irrelevant. Why risk sure profit now to "secure" an extremely chancy profit in the future?

Make sure that this occurs to him. Point it out, if you have to. You may never buy the car anyway. The car will probably end up being returned to the lessor. Why risk blowing the deal now for a profit he may never see?

After you come to terms, the store will have to call the bank or credit company to see if they'll accept the contract with the lower buyout. A factory credit arm probably will. And a bank with which the store does considerable business probably will, too. Some, however, will not. Then you simply compare the deal as it stands with the others you've found.

Note: Remember, if it costs you a bit more to buy at the end of a lease than it would if you bought in the first place, you have not "lost." The reason is that you have already gained the time value of the money you've saved through leasing's lower payments.

Buying the Car You Currently Lease

If you went and signed a contract before reading this book and are stuck with a high buyout, you can still try to bargain if you decide to buy it. Prepare as just described. Then check your contract or call the dealer or lease store and get your buyout figure. Subtract the $400 to $500 that the store has almost surely added for profit. See how the resulting figure compares with the numbers in the range you have established.

Now call the lessor and try to obtain the buyout from them. If they say they can't tell you, raise a little hell. Ask to whom you owe the money. Answer: you owe it to them, not to the dealer or the lease store. Therefore, you want the information from them, not the dealer or lease store. If they stonewall you, you can ask for the supervisor. If it leads nowhere, then it's time to visit the place where you leased the car. Your problem is that you signed a contract that includes a high buyout. No one has to sell you the vehicle for anything less.

The Emotional Approach

Offer to buy out the lease for the figure you have prepared. If they argue, tell them that you know they are tacking on a profit. Say that you're willing to pay a little profit, maybe a hundred or so, but you know they added a lot more than that.

The Rational Approach

If they stonewall you — or if you leased directly from a bank and there is no intermediary you can accuse of sleazing you into paying an unstated, "fraudulent" profit — use the argument that if you don't buy the car, no one else may buy it, either.

After all, if you won't pay the buyout price, how do they know someone else will? They don't know. There's no way they can know. They may end up handing the car back to the lessor without making a nickel. (Or be stuck with it, if they're a bank.) Yet here you are, right now, offering them a profit. And they don't have to do a thing—except give you an accurate buyout that includes a small profit, not a big one. This is a logical and sensible argument. But since you've already signed a contract, you'd better be ready to negotiate.

If you make no headway, suggest that you may be willing to offer a little more. But not the buyout price; tell them it's way too high, a ridiculous price. You won't pay it and neither will anyone else.

Will this work?

About my explanation of how to negotiate a price and lease payment, that, I can assure you, will work. If not the first time in the first store—not all stores deal, and some managers are crazy—then the second time in the second store.

But about negotiating a buyout, I can say only that sometimes it will and sometimes it won't. Your chances of making it work, however, are good. You'll be dealing with retail stores in a highly competitive business. They need happy customers. They need good word-of-mouth advertising. And they know these things cost money. On top of that, your argument is strong. A small profit now can be worth much more than a larger profit they may never see. And if you do make the negotiation work, you'll save hundreds of dollars.

Go for it.

LEASING A USED CAR

Question: Does it ever make sense to lease a used car?

Answer: It can. Consider this example. You can afford around $160 a month and you want to put no more than $300 to $500 down. You want a good, dependable car, five years old or so. You don't want it to be Neon sized; that's too small. You're thinking Toyota Camry or Honda Accord, automatic, air, hopefully tilt, cruise, locks, and windows. You look in the paper and you see that the asking prices on these cars are running from $9,500 to $10,500. Interest rates on five-year-old cars are 10 to 12 percent. Sales tax is 6 percent.

You estimate you can buy one of these for $9,000. Tax brings the total to $9,540.

This amount, $9,540, at 10% for five years is $202.70 a month, or about $2.12 per hundred dollars financed (factor: .0212). You need to remove $42 from the payment. Divide

$42 by .0212: $1,981.13. You need to put down $1,981.13 to lower your payment to $160 a month.

Even if you can bargain the price down to $8,500, you'll be financing $9,010 with tax. The payment at 10% will be $191.44 a month and to reach a monthly payment of $160.00 you must reach into your pocket for about $1,480.00 cash down.

And you really don't want the car for five years anyway.

You'll have more money three years from now and you'll be ready for something else. You look around and find a three-year used car loan for 7%.

But $9,010 at 7% for three years is $276.59 per month. Ooops.

What are your options? Older car, smaller car, lower quality car, or lease. You find a finance company that is leasing off-lease used cars. They have a five-year-old Honda Accord with forty-some thousand miles on it. You want it. What they want is $10,000; but they will lease it for three years.

How do you figure out what a good deal lease payment should be?

First, you have to find out—guess what—the actual cash value of that car. You remember what to do from chapter 8. You do it: the answer is $7,800.

You find this out despite the fact that some Web sites and some reputable car price books tell you that these cars wholesale for $9,500; you find it out from used car dealers and from *The Black Book*, and you ask the finance company's salesperson, and you challenge him if he gives you a different answer.

After you have this number, you look in *The Black Book* at older editions of this model to discover how much the car has been dropping in value every year. Assuming the car stays in relatively good shape, it should lose about $1,250 a year. Say $3,800 over the next three years. So at the end of your lease, if the car remains in reasonably good shape, its wholesale value (or actual cash value) should be $3,900 – $4,000. What will the retail price be? $2,000 to $2,400 over wholesale. $5,900 to $6,300.00, minus, of course, whatever discount can be negotiated.

Now you have the used-car equivalent of the cost and price on a new car.

To construct your ideal lease payment, use wholesale to wholesale numbers. The current cash value is $7,800. For the residual value, use your estimate future wholesale value of $3,900. Thus depreciation over 36 months is $7,800 minus $3,900, or $3,900. Divide that $3,900 by 36 months and you arrive at a monthly depreciation payment of $108.33.

Okay, interest rate is 9%. The money factor (.09 divided by 24) is .00375. Total money (7,800 + 3,900) is $11,700.

Multiplying $11,700 by .00375 gives us a monthly interest payment of $43.88. Adding the depreciation payment (108.33 + 43.88) gives us a monthly lease payment of $152.20. Plus 9.13 tax puts you at $161.33 per month for 36 months.

Now, *can you get that deal*? Probably not. You are negotiating like crazy and they keep telling you that they can get $9,000 for the car as easy as falling off a log.

Since you've done your homework, you know that they're almost telling the truth. In truth, they have no need to lease you that car at its wholesale price. So you negotiate and slowly raise your offer to $8,600.

And they take it. Good! But your lease payment can still be anything under the sun, because your lessor can choose any residual value it likes.

Your goal is to keep the depreciation low, as close to that

$3,900 as possible. Say, $4,000. Since you're paying $8,600, this requires a residual value of $4,600.

If you manage this, your payment will be:

4,000 ÷ 36 or 111.11

8,600 + 4,600 = 13,200

13,200 × .00375 or 49.50

$160.61 plus $9.64 in taxes.

Now, the question is *not*, can you come up with another $1,500–$2,000 down, to keep the payment in the $160.00 range, but instead, can you come up with $347.04 cash down to pay the taxes up front—or can you afford another $10 per month rather than $40 + per month.

NOTE: To achieve this deal, or even one five or six dollars a month higher, you will have to persuade your salesperson to write down all the figures in all the computations in the payment calculation, *as they are being done*. Why? If you look at the payment calculation above, you'll notice that $4,600 could be used to give you the depreciation you asked for, but something else, say $6,000, could be used when the computer runs the interest calculation.

And, therefore, try to keep computers out of the deal as much as humanly possible. Be prepared to figure everything out with pencil, paper, and calculator, and demand that they do the same, right in front of you.

Then take those numbers home and go over them. Don't wait to see the figures on the disclosure form when you come in to pick up the car. That's too late. At that moment, 95 percent of the people in the country, including me, experience emotions that prevent them from thinking clearly.

Also, please note that the deal we just discussed was a used car lease that we sought out. With the exception of a few Lexus and Mercedes deals, most of the used car leases I've seen advertised are about as attractive as a swarm of killer bees. Last week's paper, for example, offered a 24-month lease on a two-year-old Honda Accord LX four-door—the basic, midrange, bread-and-butter Honda—for $259 a month, with $1,517.60 down! If you can't get a brand new one for that money, or less, you haven't been paying attention.

DOES IT HAVE TO BE BAD?

Newspapers report frequently about people who have had absolutely horrible experiences at car dealerships, whether buying or leasing. But this does NOT have to happen to you. I've done many deals that were pleasant all the way through and resulted in good bargains and happy customers. The keys: DO YOUR HOMEWORK AND THEN TAKE YOUR TIME.

My happy, successful, bargain-getting customers almost always knew what they were doing and made sure they had plenty of time to do it.

Time is important. Hurrying costs money.

RESIDUAL VALUE FACTORS

Here is a sampling of residual value factors. Where you see more than one row under the name of the car, the different rows are for different lenders. One row is similar to those we used for leases financed through Ford Credit (generally, the low ones). One is "typical." The one with a star at the end of the row is similar to the factors used by the giant bank that was hungry for lease business.

The purpose of this sampling is so you can see how greatly the factors vary from car to car and lender to lender. Remember, other things being equal, the higher the residual value factor, the lower the payment.

All of these factors have been used at some time in some place. But they cannot be guaranteed accurate for your time or your place. Use them to calculate a few practice lease payments. Notice how greatly those payments can vary from lender to lender.

Note: Recently, I've noticed an "official" residual value

guide being advertised on the Internet. This is fraudulent advertising. There are no "official" residual values; there are no "official" guides.

RESIDUAL VALUE FACTORS (PERCENTAGE OF MSRP)

MODEL	LEASE TERM IN MONTHS			
	24	36	48	60
Ford Escort LX 4 door	43	37	32	
	48	41	34	28
	51	44	39	33*
Mazda Portage LX	52	46	38	32
Mustang LX	51	45	38	
	58	52	45	39*
Mustang (other models)	48	41	35	
	53	44	37	31
Mustang Convertible				
V6	64	56	47	39
GT Convertible	66	61	53	45
Ford Taurus	50	44	36	
GL 4 door	49	42	35	30
	55	47	40	35*
Chevrolet Lumina 4 door	51	43	34	26
Dodge Intrepid	61	54	45	37
Honda Accord LX 4 door	64	57	47	39
Toyota Camry LE 4 door	59	52	53	36
Ford Crown Victoria	45	37	31	
	50	42	34	28
	50	40	34	29

MODEL	LEASE TERM IN MONTHS			
	24	36	48	60
Chevrolet Caprice	47	39	31	24
Pontiac Grand Prix 2 door	53	46	37	30
Lincoln Mark VIII	52	45	37	30
Porsche 928 V8	53	47	40	33
Chevy Corvette	57	50	43	36
Jaguar XJ6	53	45	37	29
XJS V12 Convertible	50	44	37	31

4-Wheel Drives

MODEL	24	36	48	60
Ford Bronco	59	55	47	40
Ford Explorer XL 4 door	65	61	53	45
Chevy Blazer 4 door V6	66	61	53	45
Jeep Grand Cherokee 6 cyl.	65	61	52	44
Nissan Pathfinder XE	63	60	51	44
Ford Aerostar XLT Wagon V6	58	53	45	38
Ford Windstar GL	65	60	51	43
Plymouth Voyager 4 cyl.	58	53	45	37
(deduct 4% for 5 pass. seating)				
Voyager SE V6	60	54	46	39
Ford Ranger XL Long bed	61	54	44	36
(add 4% for 4WD; 2% for V6)				
Chevy S 10 Pickup 4 cyl.	59	52	42	35
(add 4% for V6)				
Ford F 150 Longbed V8	62	58	50	42
Ford F 250	66	63	51	44
(add 4% for 4WD; deduct 2% for manual trans.)				
Chevy C 1500 Longbed V8	60	57	49	41

MODEL	LEASE TERM IN MONTHS			
	24	36	48	60
Chevy C 2500	66	61	56	47
(add 4% for 4WD)				

Factors are reduced by 5% if vehicle is used commercially.

You might notice:

· The high residual of the Dodge Intrepid. If you want a Dodge Intrepid right now and can find residuals like those in the charts, go for it.
· The much higher residual for the Mustang GT convertible than for the V6 model. The difference is large enough to make the more expensive GT cost about the same to lease.

Incidentally, for conversion vans (vans fitted out like house trailers) we used to reduce the original factor by 7%. The MSRP was calculated as the vehicle's original MSRP plus the dealer cost of the conversion plus a 15% markup on that cost. Or MSRP + (dealer cost of conversion + 15%).

Again note: these are examples, intended only to introduce you to the variability of residual value factors—and thus to the variability of lease payments.

ANALYZING FACTORY-SUBSIDIZED DEALS

CHECKING A FACTORY-SUBSIDIZED LEASE PAYMENT

Let's say you see an ad for a $19,000 vehicle with a lease payment of $249.95 a month. Is it a good deal? A squint at the small print notifies you that the lease is for 24 months and requires $2,000 down. *And* there's a $750 factory cash rebate on the vehicle. For some reason, this two-year lease appeals to you. Here's how to check it out.

Get price and dealer cost.

Let's say price is $19,815 including freight "before" an options package discount of $665. Final sticker price is $19,150. You check a cost book; you find that dealer cost, including 1% for finance and advertising, is $16,585 plus $565 freight, or $17,150. Since we're constructing a good deal, we add $100 (instead of $200) for pack, bringing dealer cost to $17,250. We add $400 for profit and we're at $17,650: the sell price. We decide to use the $750 rebate as a down payment. We subtract it from $17,650, bringing us down to a capitalized cost of $16,900.

Now we need an example of a good deal lease payment. We check the two-year residual values from a few lessors for this car; we find they range from 50% to 55%. Typical is 51%; 55% is high, as with the hungry bank mentioned earlier.

We try 51%. We want a good deal, so we leave out the almost inevitable $200 to $300 bank fee and we use an 8% rate. Then figure out payments with zero down and with the $2,000 down.

NO MONEY DOWN

$19,815 × .51	= $10,105.65 residual value
$16,900 (sell price) − $10,105.65	= $6,794.35 depreciation
$6,794.35 ÷ 24	= $283.10 depreciation payment
$16,900 + $10,105.65	= $27,005.65 total money
$27,005.65 × .0033 (money factor)	= $89.12 interest payment
$283.10 + $89.12	= $372.22 monthly lease payment

$2,000 DOWN PAYMENT

Depreciation becomes $4,794.35 ÷ 24	= $199.76
Total money becomes $25,005.65 × .0033	= $82.52
Monthly lease payment	= $282.28

Compared to $282.28 the $249.95 a month offered in the ad looks pretty good.

Using the same terms, let's calculate the interest rate.

Lease payment	$249.95
Depreciation payment	−$199.76
Interest payment	= $50.19

Divide $50.19 by $25,005.65 to get the money factor: .002.

Multiply .002 by 24 for a lease rate of.0482, or 4.82%.

Okay, we can conclude it's a good rate — almost four points below what we've been using as an average or going rate — and a good deal.

Now we decide if we can find a better deal. We use the 55% residual and calculate the interest rate necessary to beat the $249.95 payment.

$19,815 × .55(residual value factor)	= $10,898 residual
$16,900 (sell price) − $2,000 down payment	= $14,900
$14,900 − $10,898	= $4,002 depreciation over 2 years
$4,002 ÷ 24	= 166.75 depreciation payment
$249.95 − $166.75	= $83.20 interest payment
$14,900 + $10,898	= $25,798 total money
$83.20 ÷ $25,798	= .003225
.003225 × 24	= .0774, or a 7.74% lease interest rate

Thus, to match the factory-sponsored deal we need a 55% residual value factor and a 7.74% lease rate. To beat it, we need a lower lease rate. So we check around town to see if we can get this deal or better on the car: a $16,900 selling price (with the rebate applied), a 55% residual value, and a 7.75% or lower lease rate. And—don't forget—no bank fee or administrative fee.

Where I am now, we cannot find that deal. No bank is offering the combination of high residual value and low interest rate needed to beat the factory deal. (Remember, lenders that use high residuals usually try make back some of the money by using high interest rates or high bank fees.) But you *might* find it where you are, so it would be worthwhile to look.

Let's say you discover that the factory-sponsored deal is unbeatable. But you don't want to put down $2,000. You call a dealership and find out if the same terms are available without the down payment. Usually, but not always, they are.

Now, you calculate the payment with nothing down. We had a $6,794.35 depreciation and a $283.10 depreciation payment.

Our total money was $16,900 + $10,105.65 = $27,005.65

$27.005.65 × .002   = $54.01
                      + $283.10
                      $337.11 monthly payment with
                      no money down

As you recall, if you can make the higher payment, you'll earn more in interest on your $2,000 ($250 to $270 at 6% for two years) than you'll save ($110 to $120).

But if the higher payment is too high, do the calculations with smaller down payments till you hit the combination of money out of pocket and monthly payment that is comfortable.

Finally, when talking to the salesperson about the deal, find out precisely what the terms are. We used a 51% residual value factor and a 4.8% lease interest rate, but the factory's credit company may be using different figures. If the quoted lease rate is significantly lower, or the residual significantly higher, do two things.

1. Figure that there's a bank or administrative fee being factored in.

2. Ask the salesperson about it when you are doing the deal.

Since the deal is good, it's not likely that you can get the administrative fee factored out. But you never know, so permit yourself to act grumpy about it. Just don't be grumpy for too long.

THE INTERNET AND OTHER LEASING RESOURCES

The World Wide Web

The Web is rapidly becoming the largest repository of information in the universe. But "large" doesn't automatically equal high quality. So when you venture into cyberspace in search of information about leasing a car, beware.

One problem is simply that the Web is a mass medium. It serves a national audience and, aside from factory invoice prices, it is difficult to make accurate assertions about cars on a national basis.

For instance, I visited the Web site of an auto buying and leasing service that claims it will save you lots of money for a fee of about $150. I looked up the wholesale and retail prices of a used car. Both wholesale and retail numbers were almost $1,000 too high. So, I reasoned astutely, if they don't know the price of the car, how would they save me money if I wanted to buy it or trade it in?

Several times in the preceding pages, I've mentioned the difficulty of determining prices and the care that you should take. I doubt that Web sites designed for a national audience can go into the kind of local detail you need when it comes to handling your trade-in. You should be able to get accurate new car invoice prices from Web sites, but, again, double-check them.

Another problem, for me at least, is that everyone seems to be selling something besides what they are selling. It's not enough to promote a book; Web sites with leasing info also feature ads for Hondas, Chevys, lease payment calculation software, lending companies, car buying services, and even radar detectors.

When a site advertises auto-related products, it becomes difficult to perceive a clear, plain, and unmistakable objectivity. For example, after visiting forty or so car-related sites, I have yet to see a mention of either Jim Ross's *How to Buy a Car*, an excellent book, or *The Black Book*, the most accurate guide available to the value of used cars. Both should be mentioned, somewhere, at least once, so their absence makes me wonder. Draw your own conclusions.

Resources Worth a Look

Here's a partial recommendation: the most accurate used car prices I found were at http://www.carprice.com. But even carprice.com will inevitably encounter limitations to accuracy imposed by local variations in value.

As for consumer publications, the *VMR Standard Automotive Guides* are worthy of mention. Their *Used Car Prices* is the most accurate consumer used car price book I've seen. (VMR International, 41 N. Main Street, North Grafton, MA 01536.)

AutoSite, at http://www.autosite.com, makes aggressive

claims about having the most up-to-date and accurate new and used car prices. Since VMR (mentioned above) is involved, maybe they're right.

At http://www.smartcalc.com you'll find an on-line calculator that purports to tell you which is the better deal: a rebate or low interest financing. I tried this example: an $18,000 car, no money down, financed at 2.9% for 48 months versus the same car with a $1,500 rebate put down on the car, resulting in $16,500 financed at 7% for 48 months. (This 7% is perhaps a shade lower than reality: at this instant (9:10 P.M.), http://www.bankrate.com reports the national average for new cars is 9.15%.) Smartcalc told me that taking the rebate and putting it down on the car was the better deal because it saved me $113.

Now if I took that factory check for $1,500 and used it to buy a 266Mhz MMX multimedia computer, I would be financing that computer for four years for an interest charge of $113 or $2.35 per month. A *good* credit card would charge $12 per month in interest. As always, the devil, and the good deal, are in the details: that is, in the specific variables that apply to you and your uses for the money.

Should You Finance a Car with a Home Equity Loan?

One Web site reports you'll save $930 on a four-year deal for a medium-priced car if you take out a home equity loan. You very well could. But the question is: should you?

What is money for? First and foremost, to make you secure. So to answer the home equity loan question, you have to consider the future. Suppose you were downsized. You get another job but suffer a 20% cut in income. Could you run into problems paying your bills?

If this is a possibility, spend the $900. Don't pile up another mortgage against your house. (Any mortgage holder can foreclose.) You can let the repo man take your new car, then go find a $500 clunker to drive. You do not want to have to find a $500 clunker to live in.

Search Engines

There are a multitude of them and they are a mixed bag. One, when asked to find leasing sites, turned up at least a hundred references to the same site. Something unholy seemed to be going on. A crossing of palms, perhaps.

Rather than list the URL's of all the search sites for you to type into your browser, here are two sites with collections of links to the major search engines: http://www.home. netscape.com (scroll down and click on "Search") and http: //www.dv-discount.com/links1.htm.

And finally, here are a couple of Yahoo subdirectories featuring lists of leasing related sites: http://www.yahoo.com/ BusinessandEconomy/Companies/Automotive/Financing/ and http://www.yahoo.com/BusinessandEconomy/Companies/ Automotive/Financing/Leasing/.

Happy surfing. But don't forget to come back and double-check everything in the plain old physical world, where the rubber meets the road and the dollars change hands. Doing that will make for happier leasing.

GLOSSARY

ACQUISITION COST or CAPITALIZED COST: Leasing's equivalent to the principal on a loan. Based on the purchase price, with various additions for fees, insurance, maintenance contracts, and any other extras you purchase, and subtractions for cash down and trade allowance, this is the amount that the lender/lessor advances the dealer to acquire the car; the price that you have negotiated to acquire the lease, a part of which you are obliged to pay back. See CAPITALIZED COST.

ACTUAL CASH VALUE (or CASH VALUE): The amount a used car can be sold for immediately; its wholesale value. Based on the previous week's automobile auction prices of the specific make and model with its specific options.

AMORTIZE: To pay off in periodic installments. The period is usually monthly, the installments usually of the same size.

APR: Annualized Percentage Rate. The total cost of your loan, including fees, points, and any other charges, expressed as a percentage rate, or an annual interest rate. If a lender charges you a $50 up-front application fee to lend you $1,000 for one year then charges only 8% interest (in an 11% market—which was what attracted you to that lender) you would pay back $86.99 a month—as if you had been lent $1,000. But you haven't; you've been lent $950. You traded $50 for $1,000, ending up with $950 more than you started with. The total cost to you for the use of that $950 would be $93.88. ($86.99 × 12 = $1,043.88 − $950 = $93.88.) Now, if you didn't have to pay back the $950 till the end of the twelfth month, your interest rate would be $93.88 ÷ $950 = .09882 or a little over 97⁄8%. But since you are paying back more than $80 of the $950 principal every month, the APR calculated on the declining balance would be over 173⁄4%. Scams like this were once common, bringing about the truth in lending laws that require disclosure of APR.

BALANCE SUBJECT TO LEASE CHARGES:

a. The depreciation plus the residual value, or the total amount on which interest is charged. Another way to look at this is the total amount of money the bank considers itself to be owed.

b. Some lenders, however, like General Electric Credit, use this phrase as a synonym for acquisition cost and/or capitalized cost.

BIG BOOK: Worth an unusually large amount. As in "the Boomer Turbo Twelve has a big book."

BOOK: Short for book value.

BOOK VALUE: What an industry standard used car price guide says a car is worth at wholesale. (Some give retail values, but retail prices are just about impossible to average in any meaningful way.)

BUMP: Noun: a price increase. Verb: to increase the price; to persuade a customer to pay more.

CAPITALIZED COST (also CAP COST): In most lease contracts, the same as acquisition cost: purchase price plus any extras or lender fees and minus anything put down.

CAPITALIZED COST REDUCTION: Cash or trade equity put down on the leased car, lowering the capitalized cost. A fancy term for down payment.

CASH DIFFERENCE: The selling price of a new car minus the trade allowance for the customer's old car.

COST: What the person selling you something paid for it.

DEALER COST: What the dealer has on his books as the cost of a car after the addition of an amount for overhead. The overhead is usually called the pack, sometimes called a "lot charge" or "lot fee" ("lot" as in parking lot).

DEPRECIATION: Loss in value due to time, use, wear and tear. Also, in auto leasing: the estimated monetary amount of that loss over the time your lease will run; and the part of your monthly lease payment which pays off that amount.

F & I GUY (a.k.a. BUSINESS MANAGER or FINANCE MANAGER): *F* stands for finance, *I* for insurance. The person at a dealership who handles customer lease or purchase financing, prepares contracts, arranges liability and collision insurance if purchased through the dealership, and, increasingly, sells the after-sale items: rustproofing, paint and fabric guard, credit life and disability insurance — and has a computer on his desk to confuse you about the price you're paying for these things.

FLOORPLAN: Dealership financing for the purchase of new cars from the manufacturer.

GROSS, GROSSES, THE GROSS: Profit on the sale of a car after its cost and the pack have been subtracted but before subtraction of sales commissions and most other expenses.

HARD DOLLARS: The amount of money, normally a portion of the trade allowance, that a dealership invests in a trade-in: the amount actually paid for a trade-in. Contrasts with SHOW DOLLARS: the portion of a trade allowance which consists of a discount off the sticker price of a new car.

INTEREST: Money charged for the use of someone else's money, which, strictly speaking, you do not pay on a lease because you are using someone else's car, not their money. This is a form of hairsplitting brought about by the legal distinctions between leasing and installment sales.

INVOICE COST: The amount the factory invoice says the

dealer has to pay for the car. In this book, we use "invoice cost" to include finance charges the dealer must pay whether or not they appear on the invoice. Sometimes known as "dead cost."

LAH: Credit life, accident, and health insurance. Insures the lender against your failing to pay due to injury, sickness, or death. Some dealerships will be kind enough to include LAH in your payment (lease or buy) without you asking for it.

LEASE CHARGES: Leasing's name for interest.

LEMON LAW: A law, usually at the state level, requiring used cars sold to the public to be halfway driveable. If it's not, the dealer is required to fix the car or take it back. (How driveable varies from place to place, as does the existence of the law.)

LEMON LAW WARRANTY: A warranty required by the lemon law on used cars. It stipulates what is covered, the amount of the deductible, and how long coverage lasts.

LENDER: Generic name for an institution that lends money.

LESSEE: The person (or company) that leases a car. You.

LESSOR: The company that buys the car then leases it to you. In most consumer leasing of vehicles for personal use, the lender is or becomes (after assignment of the lease) the lessor.

LIEN: A legal, court-enforceable claim to ownership arising

through a debt. Liens must be recorded in writing, either on the title or on some other state or county document.

LIST PRICE: Sticker price. In our terms here, MSRP after factory discounts. LISTS FOR: carries a sticker price of.

MONEY FACTOR: A "factor" is a shorthand numerical method for accomplishing a complicated interest calculation. Money factor is the name for that shorthand method in auto leasing. It can be computed by dividing the monthly interest rate in half; the resulting number is multiplied against the total balance subject to lease charges (usually the capitalized cost plus the residual value) to give the monthly interest or "lease charge" payment.

MSRP (Manufacturer's Suggested Retail Price): The amount that the manufacturer suggests the car be sold for. In this book, we are restricting the meaning to the Manufacturer's Suggested Retail Price before the manufacturer's discount(s) for options packages. If a car has no packages, or no discounts, the restriction becomes unnecessary, for then the MSRP and the sticker price are identical.

OPTIONS PACKAGE (a.k.a. OPTIONS GROUP): A number of equipment options sold as a group. The point of grouping the options is to sell the package for a kind of bulk-buying discounted price that is less than the total of the retail prices of all the options in the group.

OPTIONS PACKAGE DISCOUNT: The discount for an options group.

PACK (or PAC): An amount an auto dealer adds to invoice

cost to cover overhead. Sometimes referred to as "lot charge."

PACKAGE DISCOUNT: Same as Option Package Discount.

PIG, RAT, ROACH, SLED: Your trade-in. "Derog," as they say in dictionaries.

PURCHASE OPTION: A clause in a lease contract which gives you the right to buy the car. The time at which you may exercise the option and the price you must pay to do it are usually but not necessarily specified in the contract.

RESIDUAL VALUE: The dollar value amount that the lender/lessor expects the car to be worth at the end of the lease.

RESIDUAL VALUE FACTOR: A percentage, usually of the MSRP before factory discounts, which is used to determine a car's residual value.

RETAIL: Sticker price, list price. The MSRP after options package or other factory discounts.

A RETAIL PRICE: Any price for which a retail outlet sells a car to the public.

RETAILS FOR: Carries a sticker price of.

SHOW DOLLARS: Dealer discount off the sticker price of a new car which is shown as money paid for a trade-in. See HARD DOLLARS.

STICKER PRICE: The MSRP after manufacturer's discounts

are subtracted from the original MSRP. These discounts will be shown on the window sticker: the manufacturer wants you to be aware of the bargain you are getting.

TRADE ALLOWANCE: The total amount of discount and off price and the actual value of a used car. It is shown as an amount paid for a trade-in and subtracted from the price of a new car.

TRADE EQUITY: The amount of a trade-in's value over and above the amount owed on it.

USE TAX: In some states, leasing's equivalent of sales tax; sales tax with a different name, made necessary because a lease is not, strictly speaking, a sale to you, and lessors have the wholesale distributors' exemption from sales taxes.

WHOLESALE OR WHOLESALE VALUE: The amount, averaged within a narrow range, that a used car has been bringing at auction sales the previous week. See ACTUAL CASH VALUE.

INDEX

NOTES

NOTES

NOTES

NOTES

NOTES

NOTES